Greater London

Greater London

Michael Kilburn

Waterton Press Limited

First published in the United Kingdom in 1998 by
Frith Publishing an imprint of Waterton Press Limited.

Text and Design Copyright © Waterton Press Limited

Photographs Copyright © The Francis Frith Collection.

British Library Cataloguing in Publication Data.

Michael Kilburn
Greater London

ISBN 1-84125-077-5

Reproductions of all the photographs in this book are available as framed or mounted prints. For more information please contact The Francis Frith Collection at the address below quoting the title of this book and the page number and photograph number or title.

The Francis Frith Collection,
'Friths Barn', Teffont, Salisbury, Wiltshire, SP3 5QP
Tel: 01722 716376
E mail: bookprints@francisfrith.com
Web pages: www.francisfrith.com

Typeset in Bembo Semi Bold

Printed and bound in Great Britain by
WBC Limited, Bridgend, Glamorgan.

Contents

Francis Frith 1822-1898

Introduction
Francis Frith: A Victorian Pioneer

Francis Frith, the founder of the world famous photographic archive was a complex and multitudinous man. A devout Quaker and a highly successful and respected Victorian businessman he was also a flamboyant character.

By 1855 Frith had already established a wholesale grocery business in Liverpool and sold it for the astonishing sum of £200,000, equivalent of over £15,000,000 today. Now a multi-millionaire he was able to indulge in his irresistible desire to travel. As a child he had poured over books penned by early explorers, and his imagination had been stirred by family holidays to the sublime mountain regions of Wales and Scotland. "What a land of spirit-stirring and enriching scenes and places!" he had written. He was to return to these scenes of grandeur in later years to "recapture the thousands of vivid and tender memories", but with a very different purpose. Now in his thirties, and captivated by the new science of photography, Frith set out on a series of pioneering journeys to the Middle East, that occupied him from 1856 until 1860.

He took with him a specially-designed wicker carriage which acted as camera, dark-room and sleeping chamber. These far-flung journeys were full of intrigue and adventure. In his life story, written when he was sixty-three, Frith tells of being held captive by bandits, and fighting "an awful midnight battle to the very point of exhaustion and surrender with a deadly pack of hungry, wild dogs". He bargained for several weeks with a "mysterious priest" over a beautiful seven-volume illuminated Koran, which is now in the British Museum. Wearing full arab costume, Frith arrived at Akaba by camel seventy years before Lawrence of Arabia, where he encountered "desert princes and rival sheikhs, blazing with jewel-hilted swords".

During these extraordinary adventures he was assiduously exploring the desert regions of the Nile and recording the antiquities and people with his camera, Frith was the first photographer ever to travel beyond the sixth cataract. Africa, we must remember, was still the "Dark Continent", and Stanley and Livingstone's famous meeting was a decade into the future. The conditions for picture taking confound belief. He laboured for hours on end in his dark-room in the sweltering heat, while the volatile collodion chemicals fizzed dangerously in their trays. Often he was forced to work in tombs and caves where conditions were cooler.

Back in London he exhibited his photographs and was "rapturously cheered" by the Royal Society. His reputation as a photographer was made overnight. His photographs were issued in albums by James S. Virtue and William MacKenzie, and published simultaneously in London and New York. An eminent historian has likened their impact on the population of the time to that on our own generation of the first photographs taken on the surface of the moon.

Characteristically, Frith spotted the potential to create a new business as a specialist publisher of photographs. In 1860 he married Mary Ann Rosling and set out to photograph every city, town and village in Britain. For the next thirty years Frith travelled the country by train and by pony and trap, producing photographs that were keenly bought by the millions of Victorians who, because of the burgeoning rail network, were beginning to enjoy holidays and day trips to Britain's seaside resorts and beauty spots.

To meet the demand he gathered together a team of up to twelve photographers, and also published the work of independent artist-photographers of the reputation of Roger Fenton and Francis Bedford. Together with clerks and photographic printers he employed a substantial staff at his Reigate studios. To gain an understanding of the scale of Frith's business one only has to look at the catalogue issued by Frith & Co. in 1886. It runs to some 670 pages listing not only many thousands of views of the British Isles but also photographs of most major European countries, and China, Japan, the USA and Canada. By 1890 Frith had created the greatest specialist photographic publishing company in the world.

He died in 1898 at his villa in Cannes, his great project still growing. His sons, Eustace and Cyril, took over the task, and Frith & Co. continued in business for another seventy years, until by 1970 the archive contained over a third of a million pictures of 7,000 cities, towns and villages.

The photographic record he has left to us stands as a living monument to a remarkable and very special man.

Frith's dhow in Egypt c.1857

GREATER LONDON

Suburban villas, highway-side retreats,
That dread th'encroachment of our growing streets,
Tight boxes, neatly sashed, and in a blaze
With all a July sun's collected rays
Delight the citizen, who, gasping there,
Breathes clouds of dust, and calls it country air.

Thus William Cowper (1731-1800) passes his rather acerbic judgement on the stucco villas springing up around St Johns Wood, Camden, or Dulwich. A wave of Pooter-land houses extending outwards, the central London speculative developments of the seventeenth and eighteenth centuries, by such as Nicholas Barbon, to create the early conjoined suburbs which were to become Greater London

Although some outer fringe, essentially mediaeval villages, were affected by intrusions such as the construction of new canalized waterways in the early part of the eighteenth century, and the turnpiking of the major roads, they remained very much the agricultural settlements of earlier ages. The nineteenth century, with its industrial wealth inevitably brought with it an influx of working men and their families, who were to be housed in the seemingly endless rows of stock brick terraces of the inner suburbs, while the better off were moving to the airier suburbs of Wimbledon, Ealing and Surbiton. The suburban theatre and music hall provided relatively inexpensive entertainment, in addition to corner pubs, some with their theatres or songrooms. Most of the suburban theatres, such as the Granville at Fulham or the Putney Hippodrome have been demolished, but many of the pubs survive, sometimes with their songrooms or supper rooms intact, but hardly a one with its theatre.

With the housing also came the churches, of variable architectural quality - some, such as St Augustine's, Kilburn, were remarkable for their beauty, while a not inconsiderable percentage, were little more than utilitarian Gothic preaching boxes. Inexpensive transport by horse-bus, tram and rail made travelling into the City relatively painless, but the underground railway, as a means of transport, tended to be resisted.

The twentieth century has infilled the gaps in the landscape of Greater London, with extensive housing of the 1930's prominent in almost every outer borough, often well planned, as at Hanger Hill Gardens, and Haymills Estate in Ealing; they were the 'Little Palaces' advertised by builder John Laing in 1930. The 1930's also provided groups of notable factory buildings, i.e. Hoover at Perivale, the E.M.I. Buildings at Hayes, and the Golden Mile on the Great West Road at Brentford, along with underground stations in the up-to-date Art Deco style, cinemas such as the Granada, Tooting and public buildings, such as the Royal Masonic Hospital, Hammersmith and Hornsey Town Hall. In general terms the later twentieth century appears to have contributed little to the beauty of Greater London, but it may well be that future generations will decide otherwise.

The photographs in this book, apart from a sprinkling taken in and around central London, do not aim to record, in particular, buildings of specific tourist fame or merit: they record the under-trumpeted fabric of everyday life. Here are recorded the normal accoutrements of living; the shops, often brimming over with goods, the buildings which made up the familiar, almost unnoticed street scene, often now either partially or completely, swept away by the redevelopment of recent years, and the people, individually long forgotten, but clearly seen here going about their everyday business.

On April, 1986, Mrs Thatcher wound up the Greater London Council. Its Historic Buildings Division, a strangely non-political group of world conservation status, in a cut-throat political environment, moved under the wing of English Heritage. As a part of the Greater London Council, with the luxury of its London wide overview, and vast spectrum of knowledge, the Division fought tirelessly for Londons heritage. After 1 April 1986, it was fragmented, and its responsibilities, particularly for listed buildings in the capital, are more and more being 'downshifted' to individual borough councils, each with its own political agenda and planning policies. We cannot know what the future holds in store for the layers of delicate fabric which make up the warp and weft of Londons history - we can only wait and see.

✆ BARKING ✆
LONDON BOROUGH OF BARKING AND DAGENHAM

Saxon Berecing as developed round its abbey which, having been destroyed by the Danes, was refounded for Benedictine nuns. Although flooding in the fourteenth century caused much hardship, by the time of the Dissolution it was benefitting from a massive income of over £860 a year. The abbey ruins group well with the rather fine town church of St Margaret. From the fifteenth century until around 1900 fishing was Barkings' major industry, until the trade moved to Great Yarmouth and Lowestoft. Even the great Barking Power Station has been demolished but for its sins it has inherited a freight liner terminal.

✆ CHIPPING BARNET ✆
LONDON BOROUGH OF BARNET

Once a part of Hertfordshire, the town is situated on the Great North Road, probably originating through the market charter granted by King John in 1199 to the monks of St Albans Abbey. The attractive funnelling of the house in Wood Street on the west side of this attractive town would seem to indicate the possible site of the mediaeval market place

✆ BATTERSEA ✆
LONDON BOROUGH OF WANDSWORTH

Of its Saxon origins nothing remains above ground, and even the twelfth century church around which the village gathered, has been demolished. The present friendly, slightly New Englandish parish church dates only from the end of the eighteenth century, with a not uninteresting collection of monuments. During the nineteenth century industry came to Battersea, and the railway terminus opened at Nine Elms in 1838. Speculators arrived soon after, and streets of houses sprang up, the population increasing in excess of fifty-fold. In 1974 Covent Garden arrived in Nine Elms Lane, a sanitised version of its original home in Central London. The world famous power station - a wonderful modern industrial monument - now lies in partial ruin. Battersea Park had its brief moment of fame when in 1951 the Festival of Britain Gardens were laid out to the designs of John Piper and Osbert Lancaster.

✆ BECKENHAM ✆
LONDON BOROUGH OF BROMLEY

Biohhahema mearc of the mid-ninth century remained a relatively small village until well into the nineteenth century when suburbia began to engulf it. No mediaeval church survives, and none of the new ecclesiastical arrivals are of any particular architectural merit. The town hall of 1931 and the public hall of 1883 hardly make Beckenham a place of pilgrimage.

✆ BEXLEYHEATH ✆
LONDON BOROUGH OF BEXLEY

Developing astride the London to Dover road in the first decades of the nineteenth century, Bexleyheath expanded through an influx of industrial workers. Its town buildings are of little architectural merit, and the arrival of a massive development by Fitzroy Robinson and Partners in 1982 has done little to enhance the situation. Bexleyheath has, however, two residential gems in Danson

Park, a beautiful villa of about 1760 designed by Sir Robert Taylor, and the Red House by William Morris's friend, Philip Webb,

✆ BRENTFORD ✆
LONDON BOROUGH OF HOUNSLOW

Situated on the main road from London to the West, Brentford in the nineteenth century was considered to be one of the most squalid towns in England. An amalgam of riverside industrial development to the south of the high street fronting onto the river, and high quality seventeenth and eighteenth century houses around the Butts to the north, provides an unusual contrast. Regrettably, in the 1960s a failed architectural vision overtook the town and most of the historic buildings on the north side of the high street were demolished to erect unattractive, windswept shops. To the west of the town is Syon Park, built on the site of a Bridgettine monastery, to the designs of Robert Adam.

✆ BRIXTON ✆
LONDON BOROUGH OF LAMBETH

The Domesday village of Brixiestan is engulfed in dense nineteenth-century development. The earlier nineteenth-century residential character of the area was altered beyond recognition by the arrival of the railway around the 1860s, when smaller workers' houses began to be built along with the usual places of entertainment. In the last 50 years many immigrants have settled in the area, again changing its population mix. Brixtons most famous building is probably its prison, which opened as a House of Correction in 1820.

✆ BROMLEY ✆
LONDON BOROUGH OF BROMLEY

Bromley is the largest of the London Boroughs, but its boundaries encompass considerable areas of open land. A Saxon foundation, the Manor of the Bishops of Rochester, developed into a thriving mediaeval market town, with its charter granted in 1205. The borough has inevitably been affected by an influx of commuters, particularly after the First World War. Regrettably little modern building of any architectural value has been forthcoming.

✆ CAMBERWELL ✆
LONDON BOROUGH OF SOUTHWARK

A Domesday settlement, Canbrewelle, perhaps best known for its butterfly, the Camberwell Beauty, (now almost certainly extinct), has developed into a thriving nineteenth-century south London district. The parish church of St Giles was rebuilt following a fire in 1841, by GG Scott and WB Moffatt in an Early English style, and although there are also churches by such eminent architects as GE Street, E Bassett Keeling, with work at St Marks, Cobourg Road, by Norman Shaw, none will make the pulse race.

✆ CARSHALTON ✆
LONDON BOROUGH OF SUTTON

Beautifully situated round a picturesque pond, the archetypal grouping of the parish church, hall and pub is to be found here. Aeuueltone in 675, the name is derived from the Old English, as the village at the source of a stream, with the added self-descriptive, caese or cress. The parish church, which stands above the road, is a mixture of mediaeval and late-Victorian building, with a number of monuments, including one to John Braddyll by Rysbrack of 1753.

❧ CHADWELL HEATH ☙
LONDON BOROUGH OF REDBRIDGE

Chadwell Heath is part of that rather anonymous area of suburbia which, during the expansion of nineteenth-century London has come to physically link Ilford to Romford. The High Road is of no distinction and it has no church to catch the eye. To Nikolaus Pevsner its only claim to fame is The Furze Infant School in Bennett Road.

❧ CHEAM ☙
LONDON BOROUGH OF SUTTON

The Saxon village of Cegeham saw little of the expanding Victorian suburb of London until the early 1930s, when a better quality of commuter moved into the area, bringing the Tudoresque style of development to engulf the old village. Some of the old houses remain, particularly number 1 Whitehall, a timber-framed house of around 1500, and of the churches there is little about which to enthuse, apart from the Lumley Chapel, situated in the churchyard of the staid St Dunstans. Originally the chancel of the mediaeval building, it contains a collection of memorials worthy of note. Although now in Surrey, the great Palace of Nonsuch lay to the west of the village. Built in 1538, this amazing edifice was bought by Lord Berkeley in 1682 and almost immediately demolished. The site was successfully excavated in 1960.

❧ CHELSEA ☙
LONDON BOROUGH OF KENSINGTON AND CHELSEA

Home of Chelsea Football Club, the Chelsea Flower Show, Chelsea Hospital and ageing Slaone Rangers, Saxon Cealchyp, has become a mecca of fashionable London. A riverside village until the eighteenth century, along with the others such as Isleworth, Chiswick and Strand-on-the-Green on the north bank of the Thames, this particular area expanded with its association with royalty. Into the nineteenth century, Chelsea took upon itself an urban character, acquiring Edwardian working-class flats and commercial buildings. The King's Road brought transient trendy fame in the 1960s and early 70s.

❧ CHESSINGTON ☙
LONDON BOROUGH OF KINGSTON-UPON-THAMES

Domesday Cisendone could hardly have foreseen that by the end of the millennium, fame would have arrived at the village in the form of The World of Adventure Park, a rather unlikeable remodelling of the old Chessington Zoological Gardens. As visitors leave the Kingston Bypass to drive south to the theme park, they will hardly realise that the flinty mediaeval church of St Mary still exists, buried in a modern housing estate. One timber framed house remains in Chalky Lane but sadly, that is all.

❧ CHINGFORD ☙
LONDON BOROUGH OF WALTHAM FOREST

Chingford is situated on the edge of Epping Forest and was probably founded as a forest clearing close to the Bourne River. With the mid nineteenth century arrival of the railway the centre of gravity of the town moved away from its original mediaeval site, leaving the parish church somewhat isolated. There remains a few buildings of interest, but it is Queen Elizabeths Hunting Lodge, recently well restored, which is of primary interest. A 'standing' built to view the hunt, the lodge is a relatively rare timber-framed survival.

CITY OF LONDON

The commercial capital of England is approximately one square mile or 677 acres. City of the Romans, Londinium was the cultural capital of an advanced civilisation, about which twentieth century archaeology has revealed a great deal, and about which much has been written. To follow, in visual terms, the development of the City, a visit to the Museum of London situated adjacent to the Barbican is highly recommended.

CLAPHAM
LONDON BOROUGH OF LAMBETH

The small village of Clapham did not expand until the seventeenth century, but by the turn of the eighteenth century it had developed into a very desirable suburb. Without doubt the areas is best know for its Common, but more extensive investigation will reveal excellent eighteenth and early nineteenth century houses, and churches of interest rather than great beauty. The railway brought with it streets of terraced houses and a somewhat enigmatic character.

CROYDON
LONDON BOROUGH OF CROYDON

Situated about 10 miles south of Charing Cross is Croydon, appropriately nick-named Mini-Manhattan. The name Croydon, it is suggested, derives from 'Saffron Valley' which conjures up a picture contrasting violently with reality. The Archbishops of Canterbury had a palace here, close to the mediaeval market, but this did not prevent the town from deteriorating through an influx of workers from the woods around. The railway arrived in 1839 and the town expanded rapidly. Croydon Airport opened in 1915. During the Second World War the centre was heavily bombed, and the subsequent rebuilding during the 60s and 70s resulted in the appaling mass of concrete and glass seen today. The traffic engineer whose manoeuvrings sealed the fate of many of the town's old buildings, has markedly failed to achieve his objective: in 1998 road congestion is rife. Now the expensive Croydon Tramlink system is being built in an attempt to unblock the car-clogged town. Not a town for sightseeing.

CRYSTAL PALACE
LONDON BOROUGH OF BROMLEY

The Crystal Palace, designed by Sir Joseph Paxton and built in Hyde Park to house the Great Exhibition of 1851, was dismantled and re-erected at Sydenham in 1852, taking two years to build. Whereas the original building exhibited the products of nineteenth-century industry, here it was leisure which was at the forefront. Statistically the great nave was 1,608 ft long and 312 ft wide with wings and transepts. Terraced gardens were laid out by Paxton, who envisaged fountains rivalling Versailles, and Queen Victoria opened the building on the 10th June, 1854. In 1911 the Festival of Empire brought a wonderful array of exhibition buildings to Crystal Palace. Although fire destroyed a part of the structure in 1866, it was not until 1936 that the building was totally destroyed in a second blaze.

DULWICH
LONDON BOROUGH OF SOUTHWARK

Derived from 'The meadow where the dill grew', Dilwihs was given to Bermondsey Abbey by Henry I in 1127, the hamlet being situated around what is now Dulwich Village. In 1605, actor Edward Alleyn, who was part-owner of the Rose Theatre on Bankside and the Fortune Theatre in Golden Lane bought the Manor House and its estate, and in 1619 founded the College of God's Gift. By the mid-nineteenth century the railway had arrived at Dulwich and the rise in land values allowed the building of the New College which was opened in 1870. With the opening of the Picture Gallery early in the nineteenth century visitors came to Dulwich and in 1885 the Park was opened to the public. Samuel Matthews, the Dulwich Hermit, and Mr And Mrs Dennis Thatcher were among the villages more illustrious residents.

✆ EALING ✆
LONDON BOROUGH OF EALING

Ealing has become synonymous with film-making the world over and a byword for superb comedy, but had film producer WG Barker not bought a house here in 1904 and formed Barker Motion Photography Limited, the town would have remained an anonymous backwater. The village of Ealing originated on the north-south road from the present Uxbridge Road to the Thames at Brentford, around the mediaeval church of St Mary, which was rebuilt in 1735. The shell of the resultant brick preaching box can be discerned within the fabric of *SS Teulons* amazingly elaborate encasing of 1866. Curving roads and a few remnants of earlier houses close to the church are the only evidence of the early village. Pitzhanger Manor, situated on Ealing Green and within Walpole Park, was redesigned in 1800 by Sir John Soane, and it has recently been carefully restored by the borough council. It is now open to the public, with its particularly good collection of Martinware Pottery.

✆ EARLS COURT ✆
LONDON BOROUGH OF KENSINGTON AND CHELSEA

John Hunter, the surgeon, lived at Earls Court House before both the house and its associated hamlet were demolished to make way for nineteenth century development around the railway station. By the time the century drew to a close, the appearance of the area had become very much as it is today. It has a reputation as a part of London which provides temporary accommodation for 'comers and goers' from Australia and New Zealand.

✆ EAST HAM ✆
LONDON BOROUGH OF NEWHAM

The old English - 'Ham' meant meadow, or generally low-lying. Although now totally unrecognisable, the mediaeval church of St Mary Magdalene where William Stukeley, the antiquarian, is buried in its nine-acre churchyard, tells of a long history. The parish remained relatively peaceful as an agricultural settlement until towards the end of the nineteenth century, when it suffered a population explosion as workers from London and the neighbouring docks moved in. East Ham became a parliamentary borough in 1918 and provided Labours first two women MP in 1923.

✆ ELEPHANT AND CASTLE ✆
LONDON BOROUGH OF SOUTHWARK

Southwark or Southwork covers the main entry into London from the south, with Southwark and London bridges extant in Roman times. Inns such as *The George* and *The Tabard* have been famous for centuries, and it is here that the *Globe* and *Rose* Theatres were built in the sixteenth century. Wyngaerdes Panorama of London was here in around 1550 and Bankside was famous for strong beer and 'ladies of the night'. A visit now to the rebuilt Globe Theatre will be conducted with previously unknown decorum, while equally proper tourist venues are Southwark Cathedral and The Imperial War Museum.

✆ ELTHAM ✆
LONDON BOROUGH OF GREENWICH

Alteham grew up along the main road from London via Maidstone to Dover, and it was here in 1295 that the Bishop of Durham extended the Manor House and presented it to Edward, Prince of Wales. Improvements continued to be made and by the sixteenth century the Palace was magnificent. Greenwich Palace began to surplant Eltham in importance and by the mid seventeenth century it was said to be in ruins. By the grace of God all was not lost, and much remains to be seen, particularly the Great Hall which was restored before the second World War. Walking round this not unattractive suburb is well worthwhile, being easily reached by both road and rail.

☙ ENFIELD ☙
LONDON BOROUGH OF ENFIELD

Enfield is a very attractive market town of almost mediaeval appearance on the northern edge of Greater London, although it was, in fact, an established small village by Domesday. The rather grand parish church of St Andrew is situated on the north side of the small market place and the seventeenth century grammar school remains on its westside. Gentlemans Row, to the west of the town is one of the best streets in outer London and Forty Hall to the north, is one of the finest of the seventeenth century Middlessex houses, along with Swakeleys near Hillingdon, and Boston Manor, Brentford. The Royal Small Arms Factory opened in 1815 and the railway arrived in 1849. The 1930s brought a tide of speculative housing to sweep round the edges of the town.

☙ FINCHLEY ☙
LONDON BOROUGH OF BARNET

Finchley, derived from 'Finch Wood', does not appear until the early thirteenth century. The parish church of St Mary, a low, wide fifteenth century ragstone building is situated at Church End, but little else of merit survives in the area - apart, perhaps, from Christs College, a rather dour brick building of 1860. In East End Road is the manor House of 1723, and close to Church End is Avenue House, a picturesque Italianate building of 1898. East Finchley underground station, to the south of Church End, is a well preserved example of Art Deco railway architecture.

☙ FOOTS CRAY ☙
LONDON BOROUGH OF BEXLEY

In 1086 the Manor was held by Godwine fot, and the modern place name links this personal name with crei, as fresh or clean. The church of All Saints, which was virtually rebuilt in 1863 stands alone, close to the part of Foots Cray Place, a Palladian house designed by Issac Ware, but burnt down in 1950. A few old houses survive close to the church, while only a short distance away is the Sidcup bypass with all its associated industrial buildings.

☙ FOREST HILL ☙
LONDON BOROUGH OF LEWISHAM

Forest Hill, to the north of Sydenham, is little more than an unremarkable Victorian suburb, with no buildings of note apart from the Horniman Museum in London Road. Designed by Harrison Townsend for FJ Horniman, the tea merchant, and opened in 1901 the building contains Hornimans extensive collections. Many of the Victorian houses have now given way to modern residential development.

☙ FULHAM ☙
LONDON BOROUGH OF HAMMERSMITH AND FULLHAM

Fulham occupies the southern part of the Borough, where the Thames curves under Putney and Wandsworth Bridges. As eighth century Fulanham, the Manor was granted to the Bishops of London, and it was here that they built their Palace grouping around two courtyards. The grounds, where Bishop Compton developed his botanical collection in the later seventeenth century, are open to the public. Although close to London, and swamped by nineteenth century development, the centre of Fulham with St Johns Church at its heart, remains very much an individual town with its network of small scale streets, shops and pubs.

☙ GREENFORD ☙
LONDON BOROUGH OF EALING

Looking superficially at Greenford on the west side of London, it is very difficult to imagine that anything was here before the twentieth century. However, in Old Field Lane is the small fifteenth-century church of Holy Cross, once the centre of the mediaeval village. With its picturesque weather-boarded tower, lovely crown-post roof in the chancel, its late sixteenth-century situated glass, and monuments by Nicholas Stone and Humfrey Moyer, both of the 1630s, it is a virtually submerged gem. With the sudden increase in population in the 1930s, a second church was built in 1939 by Sir Albert Richardson, to a striking and successful design.

ᘓ HAMPSTEAD ᘔ
LONDON BOROUGH OF CAMDEN

A fashionable place to live, and the place where Boudicca is said to have died and been buried. The manor was given to the monastery at Westminster in the tenth century, and it was to Hampstead that the Abbot and his monks adjourned in order to escape the Black Death in 1349. By the end of the seventeenth century most of the woodland on the Heath has been cleared, and a race-course opened. In 1871 the right of the public to use the Heath was confirmed when the Metropolitan Board of Works became responsible for its upkeep. The underground railway arrived in 1907, and the first bricks were laid to establish Hampstead Garden Suburb, Henrietta Barnetts philanthropical dreams. Among its more famous residents over the years have been John Constable, Wilkie Collins, HG Wells and Ramsey Macdonald.

ᘓ HAMPSTEAD HEATH ᘔ
LONDON BOROUGH OF CAMDEN

The Heath is of some 800 acres, and it includes Parliament Hill, Kenwood House and a tumulus, said to be the burial place of Queen Boudicca. Medicinal springs enhanced the popularity of the area at the end of the seventeenth century, while poets and writers such as Keats and Dickens were drawn to it in the nineteenth century. Famous for its fairs, it also provides extensive facilities for horse riding and walking.

ᘓ HAMPTON COURT PALACE ᘔ
LONDON BOROUGH OF RICHMOND-UPON-THAMES

On the very western edge of Greater London, Hampton Court is one of the finest structures in England. Its building range from superb Tudor through to the splendours of Sir Christopher Wren, and the treasurers therein are spectacular. The ornamental gardens and the park with its lake have provided a succession of kings and queens with country pleasures close to London. It was Queen Victoria who opened the palace to the public. In 1986 a devastating fire in the south wing of Fountain Court destroyed much of its interior but a painstaking job of restoration was completed in 1992. A must for the visitor to London.

ᘓ HARROW-ON-THE HILL ᘔ
LONDON BOROUGH OF HARROW

Then Harrow-on-the Hills a rocky island.
And Harrow churchyard full of sailors graves
And the constant click and kissing of the trolley buses hissing
Is the level to the Wealdstone turned to waves.

So wrote Sir John Betjeman about one of the key villages in his beloved Metroland, and to anyone who has walked up through the tiered churchyard from the underground station, how accurate are those words. St Marys church, a peculiar of the Archbishop of Canterbury, crowns the hill, itself a building of considerable merit, visible from miles around. In the churchyard is a slate headstone to Thomas Port, an early fatality on the local railway line, and close by in the high street is a stone plaque commemorating what was perhaps the first fatality on the local railway line, and, in the High Street is a stone plaque commemorating what was perhaps the first fatal motor car accident. The school, founded by John Lyon in 1572, occupies a number of architecturally notable buildings grouped particularly around the church, including Old Schools, 1608 and 1821, the chapel 1857 and the

Vaughan Library 1863 by George Gilbert Scott, and the Speech Room by William Burgess of 1877. There's much to see, best out of term time.

❦ HORNCHURCH ❧
LONDON BOROUGH OF HAVERING

Monasterium Cornutum, or Horned Church, of 1228, originated around the hospital of saints Nicholas and Bernard, which was founded in 1159 to care for the aged and poor, as well as travellers and pilgrims. During the mediaeval period this small town was famous for its leather, but now very few old buildings remain. They do, however, include the seventeenth-century Old Chaplaincy, and the late sixteenth century Pennant almshouses.

❦ HOUNSLOW ❧
LONDON BOROUGH OF HOUNSLOW

Honeslaw or Hunds Barrow of Domesday, sits astride the Roman Silchester Road. In 1245 a Trinitarian house was founded here to care for the poor, and at the Dissolution of the monasteries Hounslow Manor House was built on its side - now the house has gone. Stagecoaches provided the town with profitable trade, but they also provided highwaymen on Hounslow Heath with a very adequate income, until they were caught. The Barracks were built on the Heath at the end of the eighteenth century and this fine group of brick buildings survives substantially intact. In 1919 an airport was opened on the heath, and in 1932 the Piccadilly Line came to the town. In the 1980s the unattractive Treaty Centre was built on the site of the old Town hall and library, two superb listed buildings of the early 1900s designed by local architect Noel Parr. The demolition was condoned by the borough council.

❦ ILFORD ❧
LONDON BOROUGH OF REDBRIDGE

Little more than a hamlet situated on the lands of Barking Abbey until the population explosion in the nineteenth century, its fame lay in its hospital of St Mary and St Thomas founded about 1140, for two priests, a clerk and 13 leperous brethren. The parish church of St Mary the Virgin, a Commissions Building of 1831 by James Savage is not of great interest.

❦ KENLEY ❧
LONDON BOROUGH OF CROYDON

Riddlesdown and Kenley Common were very popular with Londoners who visited them by the thousand as day trippers at the turn of the century. The Corporation of London purchased the lands in 1883 when enclosure threatened to destroy the open spaces. Population in the area burgeoned with the coming of the railway at the end of the nineteenth century.

❦ KENSINGTON ❧
LONDON BOROUGH OF KENSINGTON AND CHELSEA

Chenesitun at Domesday, it is thought that the earliest settlement might have clustered around the church of St Mary Abbots, and it remained as a small village until the nineteenth century. Market gardens occupied the southern part of the borough, while the northern part supplied hay to the central London market. The nineteenth century saw a vast increase in the population of Kensington and by the 1860s streets of 'off-the-peg' impressive but rather utilitarian houses had spread through the borough. Estates such as the Ladbroke and Phillimore built their houses and squares, but it was the Great Exhibition of 1851 which generated the development of the museums. Society flocked to Kensington, and by the 1880s it was the underground railway which provided easy access to central London. Compared to South Kensington, the north has been less fortunate, as personified in the architecturally frigid 30-storey Trellic Tower, by Erno Goldfinger of 1966. Generous patronage has ensured Kensal Green Cemetery of All Souls to be rewarding to any visitor interested in the highest class of funerary sculpture and ornament.

∽ KEW GARDENS ∾
LONDON BOROUGH OF RICHMOND

The Royal Botanic Gardens of some 300 acres, were formed out of the land associated with Kew Palace, the White House and Richmond House. The royal family did much to enhance the gardens, and by the early nineteenth century the three parts were united. The gardens intriguingly combine scientific botanic research with fine landscape falling away to the river, and outstanding buildings including Kew Palace of 1631, the Pantheon of 1837 and Sir William Chambers Pagoda, 1761.

∽ KINGSBURY ∾
LONDON BOROUGH OF BRENT

Twentieth-century housing covers much of this part of the borough, but it is the unexpected cases which raise Kingsbury above much of this area of north London. Two churches in one well-trodden churchyard make a lovely group: St Andrews Old Church, now redundant, dating from the twelfth century beside St Andrews Church which was moved from Wells Street in London in 1934. In the immediate vicinity quite extensive hedges from the earlier fields have been absorbed into the road layouts, offering considerably visual relief to the street scape. Regrettably, St Andrews Old Church is included in English Heritages Buildings at Risk Register, along with its churchyard, as victims of vandalism - a comment on society. In Slough Lane and Buck Lane are the quite outlandish timber-framed houses of EG Trowbridge, built in the 1920s from green elm, while the picturesque Row Green Village, now a designated conservation area, was designed to house munitions workers.

∽ KINGSTON-UPON-THAMES ∾
LONDON BOROUGH OF KINGSTON-UPON-THAMES

About 12 miles to the west of Charing Cross the borough rises away from the Thames to Coombe Hill and Surbiton. Cyningestun of 838 grew around the river crossing and it is the oldest of the English royal boroughs. Although remains of a mediaeval bridge have been excavated, the present structure dates from 1828. Even though it is a London borough, Surrey County Councils offices are situated in the town, and indeed the centre tends to exude a county air, rather than take upon itself a suburban quality. Oddly, there are few old buildings to be found in the town centre and these include only one outstanding pub, the *Druids Head,* with its superb seventeenth century staircase and first floor panelled room. Some timber-framed buildings have survived but only a handful. Kingston is a town which has, over the years, loved money rather than its buildings, and even now its Heritage Centre survives only on a knife-edge.

∽ LAMBETH ∾
LONDON BOROUGH OF LAMBETH

Until the nineteenth century, like much of South London, the area around Lambeth was open land linking small villages. The See of Canterbury owned the manor and by the mid eighteenth century industry was appearing, including the notable artificial stone factory of Mrs Eleanor Coade, producing an enhanced version of terracotta. Lambeth Bridge, extending across the river from Lambeth Palace was designed by Sir George Humphreys and Sir Reginald Blomfield in 1932. The borough embraces such buildings as The Royal Festival Hall, the former County Hall, St Thomas' Hospital and Waterloo Station.

❧ LAMBETH PALACE ❧
LONDON BOROUGH OF LAMBETH

The official residence of the Archbishop of Canterbury since the end of the twelfth century. Although little is known of the original buildings a thirteenth century crypt does survive. The Tudor Gateshouse adjacent to St Marys church was built by Archbishop Morton around 1495. Although war-damaged, the Great Hall with its remarkable series of domestic buildings is among the great treasures of the capital. In the churchyard of St Marys is buried William Blight of *HMS Bounty* fame.

❧ LEWISHAM ❧
LONDON BOROUGH OF LEWISHAM

Of Saxon origins, Lewisham has become one of South Londons larger shopping centres. The original village grew round the rebuilt mediaeval church of St Mary, and of the farmhouses and grander houses that were part of the expanding village scene, only the former vicarage of 1693 remains. Watermills sprung up along the Ravensbourne River, but of these only the Riverdale Mill survives behind a shopping centre. The mid nineteenth century arrival of the railway brought a wave of middle-class commuters, and the area was suddenly submerged in appropriate housing stock.

❧ MITCHAM ❧
LONDON BOROUGH OF MERTON

Industry came to Mitcham in the seventeenth and eighteenth centuries, and the turnpike arrived in or around 1745; but apart from sporadic building the area remained relatively rural until the turn of this century. With the Northern Line extended to Morden in 1926, suburban sprawl came with it. There are few buildings of merit in Mitcham, except Eagle House, 1705, and smaller cottages and pubs around the greens. Mitcham Common, an area of some 450 acres, accommodated a hunt to about 1800, Mitcham Windmill was demolished in 1905.

❧ MORTLAKE ❧
LONDON BOROUGH OF RICHMOND

Mortelaga of Domesday, probably derived from salmon stream, resides almost picturesquely on the south bank of the Thames below Kew. The parish church of St Mary retains its mid sixteenth century tower, but the remainder of the building is the work of Sir Arthur Blomfield, executed between 1885 and 1905. Although not a great work of architecture, the monuments it contains are of some merit. The Mortlake Brewery of Watneys Red Barrel fame, dominates the river frontage.

❧ NORTHWOOD ❧
LONDON BOROUGH OF HILLINGDON

The village of Northwode - literally, North Wood - of 1294 in the parish of Ruislip, lies on high ground close to the border between Greater London and Hertfordshire, and until the railway station opened on the Metropolitan Line in 1887 it remained a rural backwater. Suddenly the area became popular with London workers, and the village soon became engulfed in well-mannered housing. Architecturally modest, its great asset is Mount Vernon Hospital of 1904, by Frederick Wheeler, which includes, in the group, a superb chapel by the same architect, in the Arts and Crafts tradition. Of older buildings a fine hall house of the sixteenth century, with additions by architect Harrison Townsend, is buried among the more modern suburban dwellings.

❧ NORWOOD ❧
LONDON BOROUGH OF CROYDON.

First recorded in 1176, it was not until the early nineteenth century that villas started to appear on the high ground around Norwood. There is shopping but no real centre to a suburb which grew up around the Crystal Palace and its railway line. There is little of note by way of architecture; the churches are modest and it is only the Beulah Hill/Church Road area, with its villas from that early nineteenth century settlement that has any pretensions.

∽ PECKHAM ∾
LONDON BOROUGH OF SOUTHWARK

Pecheham of Domesday, derived from 'enclosed meadow by the hill', lies on the east-west road between Camberwell and New Cross. As with so much of this area, Peckham remained pastoral until into the nineteenth century. The canal arrived in the early 1800s, and by the middle of the century gardens were stretching down to the water. Once in place, the canal was used to carry local produce into London. In 1840, the Cemetery of All Saints at Nunhead was consecrated. Although not of the quality of Highgate, in north London, it is nevertheless of considerable interest. The 1960s saw much demolition in Peckham to allow for the erection of large council estates. The canal has been drained.

∽ NOTTING HILL ∾
LONDON BOROUGH OF KENSINGTON AND CHELSEA

Knottynghull, referred to in 1356 probably derives from a family name. Until the nineteenth century the area was probably little more than a few cottages extending along the Uxbridge Road from Marble Arch. Into the 1800s more sophisticated housing spread westwards in repeating, large stucco terraces, and by 1900 the underground railway had ensured that the area would be heavily populated with a mix of rich and poor, artistic and unskilled. In the 1990s Notting Hills fame resides in its colourful annual summer carnival.

∽ PINNER ∾
LONDON BOROUGH OF HARROW

Pinora of 1232, where the market and the fair had arrived in the main street, by the fourteenth century. Situated in the very heart of Metroland, this wonderful mediaeval village is absolutely engulfed in the 1930s suburbia of semi-detached London. The fourteenth century church stands above the high street, with its series of timber-framed houses (now shops), including a very fine hall house, Church Farm and the *Queens Head* public house. There is much to see here; around the corner from the church is the Fives Court by Cecil Brewer, 1908, and East End Farm Cottage, an amazingly complete hall house, down to a hunting scene painted on its ground floor wall plaster. Horatia Nelson (Lord Nelsons daughter by Lady Hamilton) who died in 1881, lies in the local cemetery.

∽ PURLEY ∾
LONDON BOROUGH OF CROYDON

Pirley of 1200, meaning pear-tree grove, is situated on the southern edge of Greater London, between Croydon and Coulsdon, and sits under Riddlesdown. The railway opened here in 1841, and the trains started in 1901, each helping to ease the commuters passage into London. There is no mediaeval core here, all is nineteenth century, nothing outstanding - just upper-middle-class estates and semi-detached suburbia. Needless to say its churches lack inspiration.

∽ PUTNEY ∾
LONDON BOROUGH OF WANDSWORTH

A Domesday settlement on the south bank for the Thames opposite Fulham, and a fifteenth century parish church of St Mary situated at the foot of the granite-faced bridge, which was designed by Sir Joseph Bazalgette, 1886, is one of the only building of age. In 1647, during the Civil War, a Council of War was held in the church. Pasture farming and fishing were probably the villages major industries prior to the eighteenth century, until fashion suburbia began to spread across the river. Shops and businesses extended up the high street during the latter part of the nineteenth century and the Putney

Hippodrome provided lively entertainment. The high street remains basically little changed, but regrettably the theatre fell into disuse, and was demolished in the 1970s.

∽ RICHMOND ∾
LONDON BOROUGH OF RICHMOND-UPON-THAMES

The only London borough to extend to both sides of the Thames, Richmond was originally called Sheen until the accession of the Earl of Richmond as Henry VII in 1485, after the Battle of Bosworth and the defeat of Richard III. One of several small villages along the river, including Twickenham and Teddington, its importance grew round Sheen Palace, which was demolished by Edward III and rebuilt as Richmond Palace by Henry V. The picturesque Richmond Park was enclosed for the purpose of hunting by Charles I, but today deer graze in peace and quiet. An extremely wealthy borough, it includes grand mansions such as Ham House, Kew Palace, Strawberry Hill, Marble Hill House and, indeed, Hampton Court Palace. The Theatre Royal by Frank Matcham, 1899, is superb but then there is almost something of interest in every corner of the borough.

∽ ROMFORD ∾
LONDON BOROUGH OF HAVERING

Romford is a regional shopping centre on the Roman road between London and Colchester: Rumford, or Broad Ford, is recorded around 1200, although there must have been an earlier settlement. The market grew up soon after 1200, but the church of St Edward The Confessor, by the Market Place, replaced the mediaeval one in 1850. Next to the church is Church House of the later fifteenth century, but apart from a few survivals the centre has been badly affected by demolitions since the 1960s, and by the pushing through of the ring road. Not now a town which would warrant a special pilgrimage.

∽ RUISLIP ∾
LONDON BOROUGH OF HILLINGDON

Ruislip, or 'wet place', is, like Pinner, a mediaeval and later village engulfed in 1930s semi-detached Metroland. The village centre groups in the shadow of St Martins church built around 1250, and around a very busy traffic island. Many of its buildings are timber-framed, including a find range of cottages on the north side of the churchyard, and the recently converted restaurant on the north side of the street. Manor Farm comprises two barns of particular interest; the first as a successful library conversion of 1937 and the second, The Great Barn, because recent dendrochronological investigations have proved it to date from the thirteenth century, making it the oldest timber structure in Middlesex. A rebuilt cow byre and the Manor House complete the picture, except that around the village is an enclosure ditch of which a considerable length survives. Ruislip village centre and its environs reward a visit.

∽ SIDCUP ∾
LONDON BOROUGH OF BEXLEY

Sidcup, first mentioned in 1254. It expanded in the eighteenth century and during the nineteenth century blended with Chislehurst. The railway arrived in 1866 and as in so many parts of outer London, with the railway came a housing development. Its churches have little to offer the visitor, and since the 1960s an invasion of office blocks and flats of questionable design quality has hardly enhanced the area.

∽ STANMORE ∾
LONDON BOROUGH OF HARROW

Great and Little Stanmore are situated close to the Hertfordshire border, and it is to the rising ground above the present centre that the visitor needs to look for rural quality. Up here are Bentley Priory, remodelled by Sir John Soane in the late eighteenth century, and where Queen Adelaide died in 1849, and Stanmore House, a remarkable ragstone building housing a sumptuous William Morris interior - until a great conflagration destroyed all the decoration in 1979. The interior is now absolutely plain and divided into flats. A number of buildings of interest cluster round the nearby pond. The outstanding treasure of Little Stanmore is undoubtably St Lawrence Church in Whitchurch Lane, Of mediaeval origin, the main body was rebuilt in the eighteenth century for the Duke of Chandos who lived at Canons - now demolished - in a manner so magnificent that although very small, it is one of the great buildings of London.

༄ STREATHAM ༄
LONDON BOROUGH OF LAMBETH

Streatham was a Saxon settlement, but its ancient past and even its larger houses, such as Streatham Park, have to a greater extent, gone. The rural ambience attracted city dwellers in the seventeenth century, and larger houses and villas grew up during the succeeding century. By the nineteenth century the high road was built up and by the opening of the railway station its fate as a commuter district was sealed. Much damage was done by German bombing during the Second World War and residential estates have spring up. In the twentieth century Streatham has been well-known for its entertainment, including the Ice Rink and dance hall.

༄ SURBITON ༄
LONDON BOROUGH OF KINGSTONE-UPON-THAMES

Surbiton, the leafy victim of many an undeserved television joke, is situated some two miles to the south of Kingston. Not an old settlement, it was created around the railway which Kingston had unwittingly discarded, about 1840. Coutts the bankers were generous in donating both money and land to the towns development, and mid-to late nineteenth century villas grew up, particularly between the centre, and the Thames. Many of the villas survive, but others have been surplanted by plain blocks of flats. The present railway station, 1938, is one of the first in the Art Deco style, and very fine indeed. Of its two cinemas, the early Ritz and the Odeon of the 1930s, the former is now a pub and the latter was demolished to make space for a supermarket. A few Victorian remnants survive in the main shopping street.

༄ SUTTON ༄
LONDON BOROUGH OF SUTTON

Until the London to Brighton Road was turnpiked in 1755, the village of Sutton remained rural. The settlement was beyond the first suburban expansion, but with the arrival of the railway in 1847 came the first commuters. The latter part of the nineteenth century saw an expansion in housing, but it was the mid-twentieth century that threatened to ruin the town with its explosion of office buildings, which somehow actually managed to avoid the high street. All in all, a pretty uninteresting town centre.

༄ SWISS COTTAGE ༄
LONDON BOROUGH OF CAMDEN

Situated between Finchley Road underground station and Regents Park, Swiss Cottage was so named because around 1845 one of the first buildings in the area was an inn which took the form of a Swiss chalet. Only in the last 50 years has the original been replaced.

༄ TEDDINGTON ༄
LONDON BOROUGH OF RICHMOND-UPON-THAMES

Derived from 'Teottas people' there is evidence of human presence along the riverbank since earliest times. Mediaeval Teddington, a small village, belonged to Westminster Abbey. Like much of Richmond Borough it attracted wealthy residents in the seventeenth and eighteenth centuries, such as Sir Orlando Bridgeman, the Duke of Clarence and Mrs Jordan, and Lord North. The railway arrived in 1863 and with it a veritable explosion of commuting, which in turn gave rise to a rapid expansion of speculative housing. The town is pleasant but architecturally modest - St Marys Church on the north side of Ferry Road being the highlight of any visit. Opposite St Marys is the church of St Alban, 1889, which is large and Gothic without being interesting. Further south is Normansfield hospital, founded by Dr JH Langdon-Down in 1868. In 1874 a theatre was added - a magnificent work of art and a building of rare significant. A unique survival in the English theatre tradition which in almost any other country would be cherished, but in Britain the battle to save it has been long, and its future is by no means certain.

✑ THORNTON HEATH ✑
London Borough of Croydon

Thorny homestead or enclosure, the place has long lost any such meaning on the ground. Even the highwaymen who once haunted the Heath are forgotten in this very average south London suburb. The population swelled with the arrival of the railway in 1862, but inspiration was in very short supply.

✑ TOOTING ✑
London Borough of Wandsworth

Tooting Broadway and Tooting Bec are linked by Upper Tooting Road which forms part of the main road between the Kingston bypass and central London. The derivation of the name is uncertain, but Tooting Bec formed part of the land held by the Benedictine Abbey at Bec in Normandy. Small villages until the eighteenth century, it was then that larger houses were built here, and by the beginning of the nineteenth century villas also began to appear, as did some shops in the high road. Expansion in the late nineteenth century joined Tooting to its neighbouring villages, to form the inner ring of blanket suburbia. With the extension of the Northern underground line in 1926 came stations at both Tooting Broadway and Tooting Bec by the masters of station design, Heaps and Holden. Of other buildings, the Granada cinema, with its interior by Theodore Komisarjevsky, is one of the finest in Britain.

✑ TOTTENHAM ✑
London Borough of Haringey

'Tottas village' lies to the north east of London on the main road north to Cambridge. Originally a forest village running with deer, it had by the seventeenth century become a prosperous, flourishing community and Bruce Castle, a superb manor house remodelled in 1684, and The Priory of 1620, are evidence of this affluence. A walk along the high road will also reveal a wealth of eighteenth century houses which sadly have not been well cared for within the past 25 years. It may be that the railway, bringing with it industry and workers, made the area less attractive at an early stage to those who could afford to maintain the larger properties. Today Tottenham Hotspur FC established in 1882, is its best-known product, where once it was the Tottenham Palace theatre that drew the Victorian crowds to see the stars of music hall.

✑ TWICKENHAM ✑
London Borough of Richmond-upon-Thames

Twickenham, a Saxon foundation on the north bank of the Thames, sits comfortably opposite Eel Pie Island. Prone to flooding, the church, although close to the water, was built on higher ground. Originally part of the manor of Isleworth, the village industry was probably confined mainly to fishing. Remnants of the old village are to be found in the alleyways leading away from the river and Church Street retains something of an air of the eighteenth century. Speculative housing came to the area in the eighteenth century, of which terraces such as Montpelier Row survive. The artist JMW Turner lived at Sandycombe Lodge and Charles Dickens in Aisla Park Villas. With the arrival of the railway in 1863 came a wave of commuters and modern Twickenham was born.

☙ UPMINSTER ❧
London Borough of Havering

On the eastern border of Greater London with Essex, Upminster, or Upper Church is recorded in Domesday. The parish church of St Lawrence, which probably marks the centre of the mediaeval village, retains fabric of at least thirteenth century. Other buildings in the town or close by are of particular interest, including the Clock House, 1775, the mid fifteenth century Tithe Barn in Hall Lane, and further out Great Tomkyns, a superb group comprising a fifteenth century hall house and fine fifteenth-century three bay aisled barn.

☙ UPPER NORWOOD ❧
London Borough of Croydon

Norwood, or North Wood, once occupied a heavily tree-lined landscape which flowed down into Surrey. Good for hunting, good for fuel, the woodland was also good for the provision of ship building timber. Highwaymen proliferated the area and the infamous Dick Turpin is said to have lived nearby. By the eighteenth century the tree cover was considerably reduced and by the nineteenth century the woodland was virtually no more, apart from a few remnants and villas were showing in the landscape. By 1900 the town had expanded, partly through the popularity of the Crystal Palace which was moved close by in 1854. Like much of south London the area was fairly heavily bombed during the Second World War.

☙ WALTHAMSTOW ❧
London Borough of Waltham Forest.

'Wilcumes Stow or Holy Place' is situated some six miles to the north east of the city. A small population on the Essex Flatlands until the last decades of the nineteenth century, the expansions at that time ensured its future as a truly industrialised suburb. In his youth William Morris lived in Walthamstow but he would find particular difficulty in identifying even the site of his flat pastures and open landscape. Of the parish church of St Mary, it is the monuments which catch the eye, rather than its architecture.

☙ WEMBLEY ❧
London Borough of Brent

Wembley, as an all-embracing area wears several faces, but the townscape around Wembley Park underground station which was built in the 1880s, cannot be said to be special. Much of the area was built in the 1930s with its major shopping centre in the high road, about a mile to the south west. A site close to the underground station was chosen for the British Empire Exhibition 1924-25. Originally intended to remain open only for six months, this period was later extended through the popularity of the event. A handful of the hastily erected temporary exhibition buildings remain standing after some 75 years, including the enormous Palace of Industry, a fragment of the Palace of Arts, and some evidence of the Neverstop Railway. The Empire Pool of 1934, a concrete masterpiece by Sir Owen Williams, remains in full use under its new name -Wembley Arena.

☙ WESTMINSTER ❧
City of Westminster

When Edward The Confessor moved his premier royal residence to Westminster from the City, the commercial centre of the capital became divided from the centre of royal influence. Nothing remains of his Saxon buildings, but Westminster Hall, built by William Rufus around 1100 stands as a part of the Palace of Westminster. Mediaeval Westminster did not reflect in any way the area we see in the 1990s. It was unwholesome, inhabited by the dregs of society and a place of retreat for any wrongdoer or malcontent. The pushing through of Victoria Street in the mid-nineteenth century began to reverse this ghastliness. Westminster did not receive its City Charter until 1900.

∽ WIMBLEDON ∽
London Borough of Merton

A Leafy suburb between Surbiton and Clapham, Wimbledon town sits at the foot of the steep rise to Wimbledon village and the Common. A typical late-nineteenth century commercial suburb, complete with its surviving, very active theatre of 1910, by Cecil Massey. The unassuming railway station is situated adjacent to the Town Hall façade, preserved as a sop to the towns few historic buildings, when the so-called Centre Court shopping development was built. Around the Common, over a 1,000 acres in extent, the village has a good number of impressive eighteenth-and nineteenth-century houses in a picturesque setting. The parish church of St Mary on the hill top, retains little of great age, but it is a landmark, highly visible by virtue of its fine spire.

∽ WOODFORD ∽
London Borough of Redbridge

Woodford, first recorded in 1062, still manages to blend into the remnants of Epping Forest. The not-unattractive parish church was burnt in 1969 and subsequently rebuilt. This was an area where the wealthy built and it is the larger houses which are of major interest, such as Hurst House, Claybury Hall and Elmhurst.

∽ WOOD GREEN ∽
London Borough of Haringey

Pevsner, in his *Buildings of England* (Middlesex volume), 1951, notes that the Inventory of the Royal Commission says, no monuments known, and to a greater extent he agrees. Now three of Charles Holdens underground stations - Turnpike Lane, Wood Green and Bounds Green, are well thought of historic buildings and Alexandra Palace is included in the Department of the Environment's list of buildings of special architectural or historic interest.

∽ WOOLWICH ∽
London Borough of Greenwich

Woolwich is perhaps best known on three counts, the first being the Dockyard and Ordnance Works, the second its ferry and the third that it was here that Arsenal Football Club was founded in 1886. The dockyard was established in 1512, and many ships were built here before its closure, with the loss of many jobs, in 1869. The Royal Arsenal also dates to the sixteenth century, growing to occupy a massive 1,200-acre site by 1967 when the factories closed, again with massive job losses. Many of the eighteenth and nineteenth century buildings remain, but in a deteriorating condition. The town which is surprisingly hilly has pockets of interest, but it will never be beautiful. Visits in the immediate area to the seventeenth century Charlton House and the parish church of St Luke close by, are well worthwhile.

∽ ZOOLOGICAL GARDENS ∽
City of Westminster

Situated on the north side of Regents Park and founded in 1826 by the Zoological Society of London, the gardens were laid out by Decimus Burton, the gifted architect of the Palm House, Kew Gardens and Headmasters House, Harrow School, between 1826 and 1841. Visitors flocked to the gardens to be totally fascinated by giraffes, elephants, snakes, and, in due course, insects and an aquarium. Architects of distinction have designed various enclosures, Lubetkin and Tecton, the Penguin Pool in the 1930s, and in the 1960s Sir Hugh Casson and Lord Snowden were much involved. Not only is the Zoo a place of enjoyment, but it is also one of the worlds major centres of research.

FAIRCROSS, BARKING, c.1950.   B440025
During the 1930s, London extended its tentacles along its main arteries from the City. The roads were wide, almost anticipating the future, and the buildings were modest in scale, competently designed but as with this shopping parade, boring.

STATION PARADE, BARKING, c.1955.   B440057
The view westwards from the railway station on the right, to St Margarets Church and the Abbey Gateway in the distance. Gone are the buildings on the left, to make way for 1970s replacements. Only the large block on the right remains intact and pedestrianisation has taken over the middle distance. The railway station has been rebuilt with concrete and much glazing in 1961, and it is now a listed building.

HIGH STREET, CHIPPING BARNET, *c.*1955.
Here looking north, the High Street connects Chipping Barnet to Hadley Green. Comprising essentially late nineteenth century buildings, the shopping is reasonable but the street has little to offer in either townscape terms of in architectural quality.

BARNET HILL, CHIPPING BARNET, *c.*1900.
The church of St John The Baptist dominates the street scene on the crown of the hill. Early fabric in the double north aisle dates from the fifteenth century, but the remainder of the building is of 1875 by William Butterfield, a pre-eminent architect of the later nineteenth century. The Ravenscroft chapel in the south aisle contains a fine alabaster figure of Thomas Ravenscroft, a local benefactor, dating from 1630.

TOWN HALL, BATTERSEA.

44033

The benevolent face of local government is embodied in the Town Hall of 1892, which was designed by the architect of the Old Bailey, EW Mountford. Not designed to intimidate the populous, the entrance opens onto a fine octagonal foyer. A great pity that modern council offices, such as those at Harrow or Merton exude none of this friendly ambience.

ST GEORGES CHURCH, HIGH STREET, BECKENHAM, 1899.

43377

St Georges replaced the small mediaeval parish church in 1887, to the designs of local architect W Gibbs Bartleet. The building sits comfortably at the top of the rising ground and, interestingly this photograph predates by only four years the completion of the tower.

YE OLDE WOODE HOUSE, BECKENHAM, 1899. 43376
A late timber framed mediaeval Wealden-type hall house, with its projecting wings and braced eaves. The hall occupies the centre bay, the cross passage and service wing are to the left and the high end and solar are to the right. A later inserted brick chimney stack replaces the open hall fire. The building has been lost.

CLOCK TOWER, MARKET PLACE, BEXLEY HEATH, c.1960. B650055
Although its surroundings have changed quite considerably since 1960, the squat clock tower, designed in 1911 by Walter Epps, provides a familiar marker. Of red brick and stone it is a composition of Ionic pilasters and niches above a rusticated podium. The clock face seems almost lost in the bulk of the super structure.

HIGH STREET, BRENTFORD, *c.*1955.   B400017
A fine high street of eighteenth and nineteenth century low rise buildings with, in the distance, the domed roof
of the Beehive pub, designed by the prolific local architect, Noel Parr. Disaster struck virtually all the buildings
on the left-hand side of the photograph when they were demolished in the 1960s. Today almost every one
would be considered worthy of conservation.

BROOKWELL PARK, BRIXTON, 1899.   43581
An area of rural parkland in the heart of intensive development, once created around the original Brockwell
Hall, the present house being of the early nineteenth century. The park was saved from residential
development and opened to the public in 1892. The figures in the photograph must be among the earliest
Brixton residents to appreciate the freedom of the urban park.

THE PALLADIUM AND TOWN HALL, ACRE LANE, BRIXTON, *c*.1955.
The town hall, on the right of the photograph, is a jolly Edwardian building of 1908 by Septimus Warwick and H Austen Hall, which has altered little over the past 40 years. Not so fortunate the Palladium, whose cinematic fortunes have declined to a state where this elaborate building is in nightclub use.

HIGH STREET, BROMLEY, 1899.
The almost ideal high street, with its shop windows crammed full of merchandise and its fine shop fronts under a French Renaissance façade. An impressive tower provides a distant focal point. Not so today. The large block survives with shop fronts, the tower has been demolished, and the road widened to accommodate increased traffic to and from the shopping precinct, theatre and library which occupy the left hand side of the shot. Poor Bromley.

VIEW FROM RECREATION GROUND, BROMLEY, 1898.   42940
The openness of the Kentish landscape around Bromley is well illustrated here, as a lone figure reflectively absorbs the view. The quietitude of the photograph would almost cause us to believe that the countryside goes on endlessly, instead of blending very quickly into encroaching suburbia.

CAMBERWELL GREEN, 1955.   C516005
Originally the village green, the undisturbed quality of those peaceful days had been destroyed by the wide, traffic-laden road clearly seen in the photograph. The junction is dominated now, as it was in 1955, by the impressive baroque bank with its domed corner tower, but the traffic has increased dramatically.

THREE ARCH BRIDGE, MILL LANE, CARSHALTON, 1895. 35148
An elegant but plain brick structure carrying the railway line from the south coast across the River Wandle. Although the lane has been suburbanised, the scene today would still be recognisable to the boy relaxing in the trap.

THE POND, CARSHALTON, 1896. 37669
The scene is basically little changed since 1896. The eighteenth-century Greyhound Pub on the left of the shot continues to dispense its ales, and Honeywood Lodge, an attractive house of the eighteenth century and earlier, continues to sit comfortably on the edge of the water. Further to the left of the photograph and out of the cameras view, the church of All Saints adds a considerable presence to the overall rather poetic scene rarely encountered in Greater London.

PAIRED WATERWHEELS, CARSHALTON, 1955.

C38027

In the early nineteenth century it was said that there were 40 water mills powering industry on the River Wandle along the 10 mile stretch between Carshalton and the Thames at Wandsworth. Among these was the famous Liberty Printworks at Colliers Wood, with its eighteenth-century wheelhouse and undershot water-mill. The iron and wood wheels were economical to run and, at the same time, efficient.

THE PAVEMENT, CHADWELL HEATH, 1908.   60605

The Pavement is, in fact, a part of the high road to the north of Chadwell Heath railway station. The complexion of the scene has changed whilst remaining recognisable. The buildings on the left have lost many of their decorative features, including the fine shop fronts, but the Coopers Arms pub and the former Police Station, now a pub, have escaped demolition.

HIGH STREET, CHEAM, 1932.   85088

Contemporary with the arrival of the commuter in the early 1930s. the neo-classical shops on the left and the Tudoresque on the right of the photograph, typify the accompanying quality of architecture.

CHEYNE WALK, CHELSEA, 1890.   L130084
The tide is out on Greaves Boatyard, which extended along the river wall, but in general the picture has not changed greatly. The block of houses to the right were rebuilt as Lindsey House is 1674 but altered and divided in 1775. Number 96, to the extreme right, was the home of James McNeill Whistler, the American painter and etcher and number 98 was home to Marc and Isambard Brunel, Engineers of genius.

THE OLD FORGE TEA ROOMS, CHESINGTON, 1934.   C2215001
No longer with us, but what a wonderful weather-boarded front, literally littered with contemporary advertising - in particular, a board of attractions at Kingston Empire. Along with the tea rooms, the Empire has gone, apart from its shell which evocatively displays its name painted at high level on the brickwork. Here the would-be customer strains for a view of the interior of the tea shop which can easily be imagined, with its gingham tablecloths, a steaming urn on the counter, an extensive range of cakes and sandwiches, and all standing on an irregular polished lino floor.

THE OWL PUBLIC HOUSE. LIPPITTS HILL, CHINGFORD, 1903. 50612
An idyllic shot of a rural Essex pub at the turn of the century. No longer is this the case. The building was demolished and rebuilt, not unattractively, in the 1930s. To add insult, it is now enlivened by the Metropolitan Police helicopter station close by.

STATION ROAD, CHINGFORD, 1906. 58250
Properly designed shop fronts with awnings out. Two young girls meander along the road which looks east towards Queen Elizabeths Hunting Lodge. All on the left has gone, while the building on the right are no longer recognisable. Unhappy Chingford!

TOWER OF LONDON, CITY OF LONDON, c.1890.
Built on the site of a temporary fortification, the first stages of the present building are thought to have been designed by Bishop Gundolf of Bec. The rectangular keep (White Tower) stand in the centre of the inner bailey, enclosed by a curtain wall and 13 towers. Outside this is an outer bailey wall, and a further eight towers encircled by a moat. Famous prisoners include Queen Elizabeth I, Sir Walter Raleigh, Anne Boleyn, Lady Jane Grey.

L130172

ROYAL EXCHANGE, CITY OF LONDON, *c.*1910.   L130193
The classical building, with its 8 Corinthian columns and sculptured pediment by Richard Westmacott, was designed by Sir William Tite in 1844. On the left is 'the curtain wall', the only remaining part of Sir John Soanes, Bank of England, 1788.

FLEET STREET, CITY OF LONDON, 1890.   L130080
The photograph looks east towards Ludgate Hill and St Pauls Cathedral and the street is filled almost exclusively by men in bowler and top hats. The noise of the open carts and horse buses around central London is recorded as being quite intolerable. Until recent years. Fleet Street was synonymous with the printing trade, in particular national newspapers and magazines, but these have departed, some to Wapping, leaving fine buildings to urgently seek new owners.

HIGH STREET, CLAPHAM, *c.*1955.   C327032
Only a decade after the Second World War, buildings look dreary and huge gaps remain undeveloped. Close
to the rotunda of Clapham Common underground station, the Portland stone clock-tower, some 30 ft high,
was a gift from the mayor to the people of Clapham in 1905. Its designer was Ewart Gladstone Millar.

CLAPHAM COMMON, 1885.   C327217
Samuel Pepys lived overlooking the 200 acres of common land, but by the end of the nineteenth century it had
become a place of perambulation and recreation. The photographer here displays his samples to tempt passing
trade, while in the background a shadowy figure observes the scene. Interestingly the trees are remarkably well
protected against potential damage.

CLAPHAM JUNCTION STATION.

During rush hour this enormous junction is the busiest in the world. The buildings are of several periods, beginning with those on the London-Southampton line of about 1835, followed by the line to Windsor in 1846. The Brighton/Crystal Palace section arrived in 1853. As can be seen signalling was, by todays standards, comparatively rudimentary, but computers could not prevent the Clapham rail disaster some 10 years ago.

SWAN AND SUGAR LOAF P.H. BRIGHTON ROAD, CROYDON, 1902.

A typical turn-of-the-century road house, with its multi gables and decorative pargetting. The building was new when the photograph was taken, but nearly a century on, it appears brighter and more welcoming.

NORTH END, CROYDON, 1902.
This street has a better survival rate than the unfortunate high street, and much in the photograph still exists. In this case it was the Empire Theatre which was disastrously demolished to make way for the Whitgift Centre.

48176

43

HIGH STREET, CROYDON, 1900.   46111
The High Street lies on the eastern side of the old town, comprising an attractive mix of relatively small-scale buildings, including the Grand Theatre, which was demolished soon after it closed in 1959 - an act of theatrical vandalism that was being perpetrated countrywide around this time. Needless to say, little remains in the High Street, which would be recognisable from this shot.

OLD HOUSES, CROYDON, 1890.   27824
Probably of the seventeenth century or earlier, these houses are illustrative of Croydon just beyond living memory. Even in 1890 they show all the signs of deliberate neglect and it is difficult not to see their demise already looming large.

THE PALACE GARDENS, CRYSTAL PALACE, 1890. C207020
A boating lake, a great maze and an underground grotto were among the entertainments available to visitors who flocked to Sydenham. From 1865, for some 70 years, Thomas Brock provided increasingly complex and spectacular firework displays at the site.

THE PALACE, *c.*1886.

From the gardens, one of the two 284 ft high water towers looms over the main building. The towers, sited at the extreme ends of the main structure were essential to provide a sufficient head of water to power the fountains of Paxtons vision.

The Tollgate, College Road, Dulwich, 1898. 42658

The gate was put in place in 1789 to collect tolls on the road across Dulwich Common, but the cottage dates from around 1820, with its cruciform plan and lancet windows. The rural atmosphere of the photograph has now been eroded, and a central kiosk with lifting arms has replaced the gates, but tolls still help Dulwich College in its upkeep of the private road.

UXBRIDGE ROAD, EALING, 1901.
Strangely, the scene here has changed very little since 1901. The large church of Christ The Saviour on the left of the shot, was built in 1852 by Giles Gilbert Scott, its impressive steeple showing Victorian Ealing the way to prayer and forgiveness. Although the later twentieth century has brought traffic lights, safety barriers, yellow line and a range of signs, the scale of the buildings has remained unchanged. The former Urban District Council offices of 1874 by Charles Jones, now the National Westminster bank, can be seen on the extreme right of the photograph.

E62001

THE BROADWAY, EALING, *c.*1955.   E63020

It is the lack of traffic and the casual movement of pedestrians across the road that divides the 1950s from the 1990s. The building, including Jones' Town Hall, remain little altered but a confusion of traffic lights, bollards and barriers change our perception of the scene.

EARLS COURT ROAD, EARLS COURT, *c.*1965.   E 198017

The road remains much as it did in 1965 and the photograph draws the eye towards the elegant faience façade to the station of 1915. In fact this fronts one of the finest of the later nineteenth-century underground stations, with its light, airy roof of considerable span, creating a wonderfully unconfined feel within the building.

EALING FILM STUDIOS, 1954. E63024

In 1929 Basil Dean formed Associated Talking Pictures at Ealing, and set about building the latest equipment into his sound stages. He retired in 1938 and Michael Balcon took his place, renaming the studio Ealing Studios Limited, and it was he who initiated probably the finest series of comedy films ever made, including *Kind Hearts and Coronets, The Lady Killers, Passport to Pimlico* and *Man In A White Suit.* In 1955 the BBC bought the studios but have now moved on, leaving the neglected site to its fate.

EARLS COURT EXHIBITION CENTRE, WARWICK ROAD, EARLS COURT, *c*.1965. E198009
Little altered in appearance since 1965, the building was the first permanent exhibition centre in London, when it opened in 1937. Designed by C Howard Crane, the reinforced concrete structure covers some 12 acres. The interior was much renewed in 1991.

VIEW FROM TOWN HALL, EAST HAM, *c*.1965. E100030
Looking west towards the City, the buildings in the shot present an interesting contrast between the thoughtful designs of the later nineteenth-century corner sites, and the bland up-to-date adjacent intrusions. A pity that the art of architecture seemed to have been lost in the 1950s and 60s.

ELEPHANT AND CASTLE CIRCUS, c.1890.
The meeting place of six roads, the circus was a somewhat confused junction up until the 1950s. Horse-trams, coaches, carriers and pedestrians, all with little immediate brake-power were hazardous, but to those who motor in the vicinity in the 1990s, nothing seems to have improved. The buildings in the photograph have gone and a modern nightmare has been created by, in particular, the disputed talents of Erno Goldfinger, who has given us the ugly Alexander Fleming House and its neighbouring cinema.

L130028

ST JOHN THE BAPTIST CHURCH. HIGH STREET, ELTHAM, 1961. E33069
St Johns church replace the seventeenth-century one in 1872 to the designs of AW Blomfield, with the tower and spire added later. Although it dominates the street scene it cannot be said to be an architectural gem.

CHURCH STREET, EMFIELD, *c.*1955. E179002
Virtually devoid of traffic and free of kerbside parking, shoppers can wander in relative safety. The buildings, while not distinguished, have a quality which subconsciously eases the shopping chore.

The Town, Enfield, c.1955. E179004
Close to the market place and the parish church, the weather-boarded building on the right of the photograph contributes to the feel of the centre as a market town in its own right. Although well designed as much as a high-rise building can be in a small-scale setting, the civic centre lurks just around the corner.

FINCHLEY, 1900.   F64001

In its way a classic photograph of a London suburb around the turn of the century, with a mix of design and scale in the roadside building. Shopfronts with their windows full of merchandise and a certain unhurried atmosphere presents a picture of life far removed from the urgency of the late twentieth century.

HIGH STREET, FOOTS CRAY, 1900.   45834

As children pose unconcernedly along the street, it is difficult not to feel that the quality of life in 1900 has much to teach us at the Millennium. Although it is the main road, the high street is narrow, giving it an enclosed almost medieval character.

DEVONSHIRE ROAD, FOREST HILL, 1898.   42673

The view down Devonshire Road remains recognisable from the photograph, and the United Reformed Church of St John still acts as an attractive focal point. Designed in 1884 by JT Barker, it is spacious with its angel head hammer-beam roof, making a valuable contribution to an otherwise under-decorated interior.

FULHAM BROADWAY, *c*.1965.   F69028

The junction now pulsates with traffic, but the buildings remain little altered. The key building in this part of Fulham is the town hall, seen here in the distance: a fine Italianate edifice recently sympathetically restored by the borough council.

FULHAM BROADWAY, FULHAM, 1900.

F69001

This view has changed more than any other in the town centre, through the loss of the Granville Theatre, seen here on the left, a masterpiece by Frank Matcham of 1898. Making a decision amounting to wilful planning vandalism, Hammersmith Borough Council, against the advice of the Greater London Councils Historic Buildings Board, granted consent to demolition it in 1971. The replacement building, a little admired office block, occupies the site, complete with a very strange piece of sculpture, which must have been provided in an attempt to add interest to the site.

GREENFORD ROAD, GREENFORD, c.1965.

G242006

This view, which has, in essence, changed very little since 1965, sums up the character of Greenford: all of the 1930s, small scale and generally, uninteresting. Not an area which would invite any driver to park his car and investigate further.

HIGH STREET, HAMPSTEAD, 1889.   41570
The photograph looks from the High Street towards Holly Hill, and on to West Heath. The pleasant shop
fronts have gone, but the buildings remain, including the Old Fire Station with its prominent tower.
Regrettably, its original use has been surplanted by offices and the upper part of the tower above the clock, has
been removed. Perhaps one day it will be rebuilt.

THE OLD BULL AND BUSH, NORTH END WAY, HAMPSTEAD HEATH, 1898.   41581
The pub is said to have been built as a farm in the mid seventeenth century, and it was licensed in 1721. It is
alleged to have been the home of William Hogarth, the painter. Among its known drinkers were Thomas
Gainsborough, Joshua Reynolds and David Garrick. The building as seen in the photograph appears as an
atmospheric drinkers dream, with its low doorway probably stepping down into a dark panelled bar with its
smoke-stained ceiling.

THE OLD BULL AND BUSH, NORTH END WAY, HAMPSTEAD HEATH, 1965. G271043
The earlier pub, made famous by music hall star Florrie Ford, was demolished in the early 1920s, and rebuilt to a vaguely similar design. The bay windows of the old pub are echoed with sash windows above, but the new building is inescapably of its period. Internally some of the old features have been retained and additionally there are good inter-War fittings.

EAST FRONT, HAMPTON COURT, 1889. 43046
The King's Rooms and the Queen's Rooms refer to William and Mary, and it is the Queens Chambers that occupy the east front. Coming to the throne in 1668, William considered the palace to be old fashioned and out of date. Thus up-to-date architect Sir Christopher Wren, a latter-day Richard Rogers, was engaged to rebuild the Palace from scratch, but luckily the task was never completed. Grinling Gibbons and ironworker Jean Tijou were among the artists and craftsmen who decorated the interior and exterior of the new work.

THE RIVER THAMES, HAMPTON COURT, PALACE, 1896. 38341

A hundred years after the photograph was taken, visitors to Hampton Court generally arrive by rail, road or on foot. While some still do make the journey by river, it is not the common form of transport. The picturesque paddle steamer and the river bank dropping into the water have unhappily been surplanted by motor boats and a river wall which gives the water a hard demarcated edge.

HIGH STREET, HARROW-ON-THE-HILL, 1906. 53630

It is surprising how little the high street has changed from this viewpoint since 1906. The shops closest to the camera have gone to become offices, but then so many shops have gone from the hill, as dormitory residents go to the local supermarkets. The slow withdrawal of shopping from the village is not a new phenomenon, in fact it began at least before the turn of the century when those on the western slope became houses, leaving only their large windows as evidence on an earlier use. Appearances can sometimes be deceptive, and the origins of the row of buildings closest to the camera are buried within the fabric.

STATION ROAD, HARROW-ON-THE-HILL, 1914.   66820
The building on the left remain extant but in a changed form, particularly at ground floor level. How peaceful life appears in what must have been a time of agitation as the Great War loomed over Europe.

HIGH STREET, HORNCHURCH, 1909.   62081
A wide picturesque and peaceful high street, as it was prior to the arrival of huge numbers of Londons commuters. The buildings on the left of the photograph were completely replace in the 1950s - 70s, and those on the right have also gone. Only the Bull public house remains, but in a rebuilt state.

NORTH STREET, HORNCHURCH, 1908.   59856
This view looks up North Street to what is now the main focus of the town, *The Queens Theatre*. All the buildings in the photograph have gone, being replaced by 1930s development. St Andrews Church House seen in the distance still stands but denuded of its spirelet.

STAINES ROAD, HOUNSLOW, *c.*1965.   H162001
The Staines Road has remained a thoroughfare of small scale development, until it reaches Hounslow town, where higher buildings intrude. In the main, a townscape absorbing the late-nineteenth and early twentieth century spread of the suburbs.

BELL JUNCTION, HOUNSLOW, 1955.   H162016
It is difficult to find any virtues in this flat high street. Extending eastwards from Bell Junction to the rather nasty bus station, its recent pedestrianisation has done nothing to add to its lack of attraction.

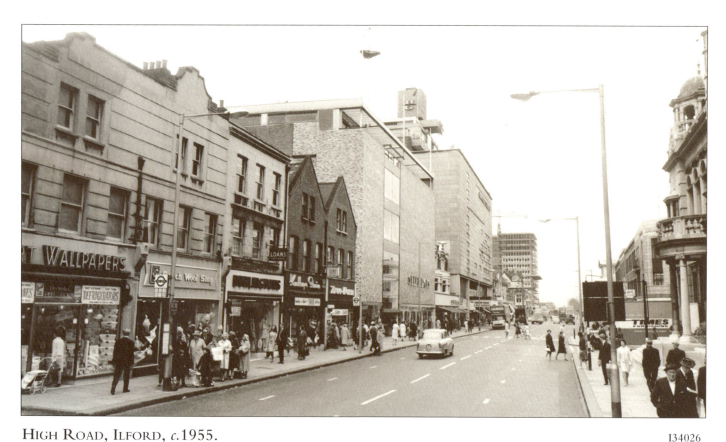

HIGH ROAD, ILFORD, *c*.1955.   I34026
Two buildings in this shot are of particular interest. The town hall on the extreme right by Wolland in a free classical style, and Harrison Gibsons' Store in the centre of the photograph. The original building was burnt in the 1960s and rebuilt at remarkable speed which may or may not account for its rather odd design.

RIDDLESDOWN TEA ROOMS, KENLEY, 1903.   50542
Although billed as the Riddlesdown Tea Rooms, it was in fact Gardeners' Pleasure Resort which attracted the trippers. Here was a zoo, a museum, a narrow gauge railway and refreshment rooms on a small scale. Although the in use disappeared long ago, the house remains in an altered state as number 23, Godstone Road. The sashed windows have been replaced, the roof covering has changed and the railway-style bargeboard and finial have gone.

KENSINGTON PALACE, SOUTH FRONT, 1899.   43594
The Palace was originally built in 1605 as a relatively small house for Sir George Coppin, but it was William and Mary who enlarged it as a quiet residence in the virtual countryside. The south front of 11 bays dates from about 1695, when Sir Christopher Wren was in charge of the works. Now a bronze statue of William III stands in front of the building, a present to Edward VII from Kaiser Wilhelm II.

KENSINGTON PALACE, THE KINGS GALLERY, 1899. 43831
The gallery extends along the south front of the palace for some 95 ft. It is a beautiful room which has changed little since 1899. The photograph must have been taken soon after its restoration in that same year.

KENSINGTON PALACE, EAST FRONT, 1899. 43592
Looking out onto Dial Walk, this elevation dates from 1629, but it was improved as part of the rebuilding works completed in 1726. In the foreground the statue of the seated Queen Victoria, in white marble on a Portland stone base, is by Princess Louise 1887.

KENSINGTON CHURCH STREET, 1906.

K9023

The Serpentine curves of Kensington Church Street betray the origins of this mediaeval road, which ran between the village around St Mary Abbots, and Notting Hill to the north. By the beginning of the nineteenth century the area was a fashionable West London place of residence, with royal patronage, and known as 'Imperial Kensington'. The aristocracy migrated here and for this reason anyone at all given to establishing a place in society, followed.

HIGH STREET, KENSINGTON, 1899.
Horse-buses and wagons hurry past a very isolated policeman. The buildings all appear to be of the nineteenth century with the traditional corner pub beautifully decorated with flowers at every window. Sadly for London, all this has been demolished to make way for much that is of the 1930s.

K9024

PALACE GARDENS TERRACE, KENSINGTON, 1906.   55475
The photograph looks towards Inverness Gardens, and the buildings on either side of the road are perfect examples of the mid nineteenth century spread of impressive stucco cliffs over much of Kensington and Westminster. Standard mouldings make up the porches, windows and cornices. The plan of every house is a repeat of its next-door neighbour resulting in reasonably attractive but repetitive architecture.

THE PALM HOUSE, KEW GARDENS, 1899.   43756
Designed by architect Decimus Burton and engineer Richard Turner, the Palm House was completed in 1848, a supremely elegant exercise in wrought iron and glass, 362 ft long and, at its highest point, 62 ft. The huge curving panels of glass add to the wonder of this structure.

KINGSBURY ROAD, KINGSBURY, *c.*1960.   K142028
A busy shopping street with buildings of human scale of the 1920s and 30s, with a prominent well-designed
Midland Bank sign, now replaced by ugly symbols.

SWIMMING POOL, KINGSBURY, *c.*1955.   K142054
The Kingsbury pool was large by municipal standards and was situated on the edge of Roe Green Park. The
Art Deco buildings were elegant, but along with so many other outdoor pools all over Britain, it has been
demolished.

VIEW FROM KINGSTON BRIDGE, KINGSTON-UPON-THAMES, 1896.   38322
Look down from the bridge in the 1990s and in the main all that is likely to be seen is murky water and a few
ducks. Such a lively scene as the one in the photograph is very much of the past, when almost unbelievably,
the river drew vast crowds and boating was a popular pastime.

ALL SAINTS CHURCH FROM CLARENCE STREET, KINGSTON-UPON-THAMES, 1906.   54715
A rather grand town church, beautifully situated close to the Market Place, and although older it looks to be
of the later fourteenth century. The brick top to the tower, recently restored, is of 1708. The church has some
nice monuments, including one to Phillip Meadows by Flaxman, 1795, and a seated figure of Louisa Theodosia,
Countess of Liverpool by Chantry, 1825. The railings in front of the church presumably went with all good
intentions to aid the war effort c.1940. The buildings on the left have been demolished.

THE MARKET PLACE, KINGSTON-UPON-THAMES, 1906. 54707

The triangular market place and its adjacent alleyways give a realistic impression of age, but apart from the layout little fabric predates the nineteenth century. The photograph shows market stalls exceeding todays numbers clustered around the rather dull looking Market House of 1840. Recently the building has received a welcome clean and the lead statue of Queen Anne, 1706, on its balcony front has been regilded - a plus mark for Kingston!

HIGH STREET, KINGSTON-UPON-THAMES, 1906. 54709

Except for its front wall the Griffin Hotel has gone, in order to build a shopping mall in the 1980s. The so called Kings Stone in the foreground has been moved and the buildings on the right have been demolished. This very much accords with the ongoing story of Kingston, as yet another development is anticipated on the river frontage.

THE HOGS MILL WATERSPLASH, KINGSTON-UPON-THAMES, 1906.   54725
At the end of the nineteenth century, the Watersplash was situated at, what is now Bedelsford Bridge, close to the former Hodgsons Kingston Brewery. Once producing 1.5 million gallons of beer a year, the site is now occupied by yet more of the towns money spinning office blocks. Soon a huge percentage of office workers will operate from home through the Internet and what will happen to these gross, ugly buildings then?

RIVERSIDE, LAMBETH, *c.*1880.   L130120
Slums and industry invaded Lambeth during the nineteenth century, with little clearance until the 1900s. These houses could well have come from the vivid descriptions of riverbank existence in Dickens, *Our Mutual Friend*. The area is now replaced by smart, clean office blocks.

LAMBETH PALACE AND ST MARYS CHURCH, 1900.   L130139
The popularity of the river at the turn of the century is here for all to see. The pleasure boats filled with trippers plied their trade from Greenwich to Hampton Court with, as the photograph shows, a pick up, put-down point at Lambeth pier.

UPPER GREEN, MITCHAM, *c*.1960.   M296057

The camera looks towards St Marks Road and Upper Green East. In 1960, the Kings Head public house on the left and the Art Deco Majestic Cinema grouping with the Green make an ideal combination. Although the pub and the Green survive, the cinema site now accommodates a fast-food restaurant - a sign of the times.

HIGH STREET, LEWISHAM, *c*.1960.   L373013

The High Street of 1960 remains surprisingly recognisable. The buildings behind the clock tower are, in the main, extant, as it the Italian style campanile to the church of St Saviours, which was added in 1929. The Burton building on the right of the shot has been demolished to allow the formation of the entrance to a recent shopping mall. The odd phenomena in the street is the fact that the council took down and rebuilt the clock Tower a few feet to the right of its original site in order to accommodate the realignment of roads and a pedestrianisation scheme. The clock tower was built to celebrate the Diamond Jubilee of Queen Victoria in 1897.

HIGH STREET, MORTLAKE, *c.*1955. M279001
Apart from an increase in its volume of traffic, the street scene has changed little as White Hart Lane meets the high street. The architecture is hardly lively – in fact, it could be said to be somewhat depressing.

MAXWELL ROAD, NORTHWOOD, 1903. 49316
Close to the Metropolitan railway station, Maxwell Road links the main shopping street to Rickmansworth Road. The shops in Northwood seem to be consciously aimed at the young city worker and those away from the centre, and in the shadow of the supermarket probably find the going more difficult.

WESTOW HILL, NORTHWOOD, 1898.   42645
At the end of the nineteenth century Westow Hill, was an upper middle class shopping street, rising up in the photograph to focus on one of the great water towers at Crystal Palace.

QUEENS ROAD, PECKHAM, c.1955.   P289011
The camera looks east towards New Cross Gate. Early mid nineteenth century buildings line Queens Road at its junction with Montpelier Road. Here, in 1955, was much Victorian architecture awaiting the clearance of the 1960s.

HIGH STREET, NOTTING HILL, *c.*1890.   8235
No longer the high street, now part of Notting Hill Gate. The four-storey stucco terrace must have been about 40 years old when the photograph was taken. The repetitive nature of the buildings in the area around Notting Hill does not encourage long exploratory walks.

BRIDGE STREET, PINNER, *c.*1955.   P296012
Behind the bus and to the left is the high street of remarkable beauty, but the camera records this mundane street scene, which has changed little since 1955. It is busier now, with more street signs and a supermarket, but the villages desire to somehow remain 'untouched' is strong.

HIGH STREET, PURLEY, 1903.   49445
In 1900 there were only seven shops on the high street, and one on Brighton Road, but by the outbreak of the
Second World War there had been a dramatic increase. Development in the area was carried out by one man,
JP Oldaker, who was responsible for the buildings on the left of the photograph, Mafeking Terrace was
completed in 1900. The school to be seen beyond the terrace has been demolished.

FROM PURLEY DOWNS. 1903.   49438
The landscape of rural Surrey stretches away behind a layer of early twentieth century suburbia lapping around
Purley. A garden suburb-type estate of around this date was being laid out near Woodcote Village by William
Webb and aimed at the more affluent buyer.

BRIGHTON ROAD, PURLEY, 1903. 49450

Croydon Corporation trams came to Purley in 1901, and were phased out in 1951, making way for buses. Although the buildings on the left of the photograph remain standing, albeit with simplified shop fronts, the area has been developed. The road in 1903 is not deserted, but now it veritably buzzes with activity.

THE BARREL ORGAN, PUTNEY, 1900. P332030

Contrasting with the tinkling of the harpsichord of Beau Nash's Georgian Bath, here is the music of the late nineteenth century streets. Itinerant musicians, often making only a meagre living, eking out their daily life, and bringing with them more pleasure that we, in this 24-hour music age, can now imagine. In todays London, the same musical tradition can be regularly seen: the street musician, probably with a violin, a saxophone or maybe a trumpet, some dreadful, some gifted, always brightening up the day.

HIGH STREET, PUTNEY, *c.*1965. P332010
It is at the river end of the high street that most changes have taken place over the past 30 years. The buildings on the left of the photograph are substantially intact, but apart from the church, the Palace and the Regal and all the other buildings have been demolished. Faceless office blocks now occupy this run of street, and one signal cinema has been shoe-horned into the new development.

GEORGE STREET, RICHMOND, *c.*1955. R31076
Here on film is a record of everyday life in Richmond town centre around 1955. The camera looks past the right-hand turning into Sheen Road, towards the railway station. Forty years have failed to change this townscape to any great extent, but traffic now jams the street, and fashions have changed dramatically. The town looks strangely brighter in 1998.

THE MARKET PLACE, ROMFORD, 1908.
The street market remains into the 1990s, but gone are the animals that used to be a part of the scene. Gone also is Laurie Hall, the building which, in the photograph stops the market place, demolished some 25 years ago. Church House on the extreme left of the shot remains, but almost next door is the Romford Shopping Mall, matched on the right by the Romford Shopping Centre.

ROMFORD BREWERY, 1908.
Situated on the south side of the high street, the exact date of the founding of the brewery is not known, but a dated chimneypiece of 1799 is to be found in the main entrance hall. Most of the extant buildings fronting the high street appear to be of the late-nineteenth or early-twentieth century, but of the buildings in the photograph few remain. In 1998 discussions are proceeding with the borough council regarding the possible redevelopment of the site for housing, shops and offices. The founder of the brewery was Mr Ind, a local man, who later became a partner to Mr Coope.

SOUTH STREET, ROMFORD, 1908.   59808
Tremendous lanterns and shop fronts of the like we rarely see today. This part of Romford, here focusing on
the Golden Lion pub, with its eighteenth century front masking a seventeenth-century interior, has been
generally detrimentally affected by pedestrianisation schemes.

RUISLIP LIDO, RESERVOIR ROAD, c.1965.   R335077
The lido is situated about one mile to the north of Ruislip village. The grounds were laid out by TH Mawson,
1936, during the era of outdoor pool building, and in this context the lido is rather special on account of its
grand scale. The main building, a find Art Deco design by GW Smith, is now altered reasonably sympathetically into a pub, but the miniature railway track which skirted the waters edge on the opposite bank remains as
something of a reminder of those balmy pre-war days.

HIGH STREET, SIDCUP, *c.*1965.   S127106
Sidcup High Street was uninspiring in 1965, and so it remains.

FROGNAL AVENUE, SIDCUP, 1900.   45823
A tranquil country road in 1900, now, although the road is little changed, the Sidcup bypass roars by to the left of the photograph. On the right is the gated entrance to Frognal House, with its remains of building periods from late mediaeval through to the eighteenth century. The turret showing through the trees, crowns the stable block, dating also from the eighteenth century. Idyllic it could have been, had the area health authority not allowed it to go to ruin during the 1970s against all the advice of The Greater London Council. The stable block has now been demolished and the house has lost a high percentage of its historic interest.

THE BROADWAY, STANMORE, 1906. 55690
The Broadway is now a faceless sort of place, apart from a long row of later sixteenth-century jettied cottages, and a well-disguised Hall House of around 1500. It lacks grace or inspiration in its buildings and relief can only be gained at its western end through the high-walled Bernays Gardens, or through the churches of St John the Evangelist - two buildings in one churchyard, one of around 1849, the other a beautiful brick ruin of around 1630.

HIGH ROAD, STREATHAM, 1898. 42785
The photograph looks south at the junction of the High Road with Mitcham Lane, The church of St Leonard marks the centre of the mediaeval village, with its fourteenth century tower crowned by a broach spire of 1841. The church holds a comprehensive collection of monuments. Apart from inevitable modifications and alterations, including the introduction of traffic lights, the scene remains much as the photograph. The drinking fountain in the foreground was given by William Dyce, a painter, in 1862.

QUEENS PROMENADE, SURBITON, 1896. 38333

Subtle changes have altered this view form the Hampton Court towpath. Trees have grown up to form a green barrier between the Promenade and the busy Portsmouth Road running parallel behind it. Some of the villas along the river have survived, but expensive apartments have replaced a number of the others.

LONDON PROVINCIAL BANK. HIGH STREET, SUTTON, 1900. 45478

Now a Barclays branch, the bank designed in a French Renaissance style occupies the angle between the High Street and Cheam Road. Over the years it has changed very little. It has lost its ornamental gables above the triple light dormer windows, and the Royal Dairy shop front has been removed and replace by two arched openings which match the original three.

THE COCK HOTEL. HIGH STREET, SUTTON, 1890. 27423A

The earlier Cock Hotel selling beer and spirits out of its eighteenth-century building. Although not entirely rural, it exudes a quality which drinkers would travel a long way to sample in 1998. Around 1800 the Cock was a favourite stopping place for the London to Brighton stagecoach.

THE COCK HOTEL, HIGH STREET, SUTTON, 1898. 41708

What a difference eight years can make! The Old Cock has been discarded and the brewery prepares for the twentieth century with an up-to-the-minute design. Somewhat ironically this building has, in its turn, been demolished in 1961 and all that has remained to mark its passing is the post sign on an island in the middle of the High Street.

HIGH STREET, SUTTON, 1932.   85078
The Austin Seven in the foreground of the photograph is probably as interesting as anything in the high street. Although the street did survive in a reasonable state until the 1960s, it has now become a fairly ordinary run of commercial buildings and shops.

NORTHWAYS PARADE, FINCHLEY ROAD, SWISS COTTAGE, 1965.   S650008
The block of flats and shops, all embracingly called Northways Parade, is situated to the north of Swiss Cottage underground station. Apart from a particularly intrusive advertisement which now bridges the gap between New College Parade on the extreme left and Northways Parade, the buildings have changed very little. Finchley Road is now a Red Route into the city, with safety barriers down the middle. It is now wide, but not particularly fast. Northways Parade is of the 1930s, and although heavy, the blocks are well detailed.

THE ANGLERS HOTEL, TEDDINGTON, 1890.   23538
Close to Ferry Road and Teddington Lock, the Anglers Hotel has always been a popular venue. Not only is it well placed to attract those enjoying the river, but also the army of employees from the neighbouring television studios.

TEDDINGTON LOCK, 1899.   43054
The lock and weir mark the highest point in the Thames to which medium tides flow. The weir was built in 1811 to improve river navigation and the lock shown in the photograph, in 1857. The rollers, close to the camera, were placed to allow small craft to be literally rolled over, while in the centre of the shot is the skiff lock, designed to accommodate medium sized craft. To the right is the barge lock. This group was demolished and re-built in 1950. Behind the camera is an elegant suspension bridge installed in 1888, allowing foot traffic between Teddington and Ham.

HIGH STREET, THORNTON HEATH, c.1955.   T262007
The tram, almost at the end of its useful life, adds interest to the otherwise bland junction between the high street and Grange Road. The photograph would have been considerably cheered up by the inclusion of St Albans church, just off camera to the right, which was the first church designed by the great Sir Ninian Comper, in 1894.

THE COMMON, TOOTING BEC, 1898.   42798
Some 150 acres in area, the Common extends north-south from Balham to Streatham Park, and onto the smaller Tooting Graveney Common. Rather than presenting the observer with an impression of the countryside in London, the photograph exudes an air of watery municipality.

TOOTING BROADWAY, *c*.1955.

An unremarkable suburban junction is relieved by the presence of a fine bronze standing figure of Edward VII by LF Roselieb, 1911, on a granite plinth adorned by plaques of *Charity* and *Peace*. Behind the statue is a superb late nineteenth-century cast iron ventilator gas standard above the public lavatory. The ornate candelabrum with its foliate branches has been restored since 1955 and its lanterns have been replaced.

LORDSHIP LANE, TOTTENHAM, 1903.

The view looks east to west to Lordship Lane school in the distance, with the buildings on the right temporarily stemming the flow of suburbia from the north. The new road has been set out and Westbury Avenue will be built up in the meadow within a relatively short space of time. This is an interesting shot taken at the moment of the areas transition from semi-rural to full blown Edwardian suburbia.

THE EMBANKMENT, TWICKENHAM, 1890.   23535
A valuable photographic record of what was once Twickenhams riverside, until Second World War bombs
dropped and obliterated this part of the town. All that survives is the house on the extreme right of the shot,
with the decorative doorcase now removed to the opposite end of the façade. The area is, to some extent
occupied by a car park.

EEL PIE ISLAND, TWICKENHAM, 1899.   43741
Eel Pie Island, was a popular stopping-off point for riverboat trippers. The name recalls a long dead industry,
although the hotel on the island in the middle of the last century, may well have tried to keep the tradition
alive. A footbridge now gives access to the island and houses have replaced the hotel. Although the bones of
the photograph remain, the flesh has been remodelled. The islands later twentieth century claim to fame is as
a venue for early Rolling Stones concerts.

KING STREET, TWICKENHAM, 1909.   T91001
The street swings to the left towards the railway station, with the then new stone-faced Italianate bank dominating the junction. Late eighteenth century buildings front the street on the left, while earlier shops survive on the right. In 1909 the bank must have been a remarkable intrusion into a red brick streetscape.

KING STREET, TWICKENHAM, c.1960.   T91039
Fifty years have taken a subtle toll on the architecture of this junction. The bank survives unscathed, but the early buildings have now, in the main, been demolished to make way for up-to-date modern 'Georgian'. The good street furniture of 1909 has also gone to be replaced by characterless 1950s borough council lighting. All forward looking in concept but retrogressive in implementation.

T91046

THE RUGBY GROUND, WHITTON ROAD, TWICKENHAM, *c.*1960.
'Billy Williams Cabbage Patch', was purchased in 1907, and opened in 1909, following the erection of the east and west stands, which allowed the ground to accommodate some 30,000 spectators. Slowly the buildings were expanded during the early 1930s until the 1980s and 90s saw the erection of overpowering, almost brutalist stands designed by Howard Lobb and Partners. Not a beautiful sight from the roads around but they seem to do the job perfectly wells.

59867

UPMINSTER WINDMILL, ST MARYS LANE, UPMINSTER, 1908.
The highlight of a visit to the town must be this weatherboarded octagonal smock mill, supported on its brick base. In use until 1934, the photograph shows four double-shutter patent sails and a boat shaped cap with fantail. Internally its machinery has recently been restored. The Mills' survival was in theory guaranteed, first by Essex County Council, and then by the borough council but now the structure is entered on English Heritages Buildings At Risk Register, a very sad state of affairs indeed.

WESTOW HILL, UPPER NORWOOD, *c*.1955.
U42006
This view looking westwards towards the spired United Reformed, now Greek Orthodox church of 1878 and the library is readily recognisable. Needless to say few of the well-designed shop fronts survive.

HIGH STREET, UXBRIDGE, *c*.1955.
U52015
The camera looks east towards the lovely Market Hall with its clock turret, along a fine street of eighteenth-century and earlier houses. Soon the buildings on the right, close to the camera, would be demolished to accommodate a diabolical shopping precinct, which has in recent years been given a much-need facelift. Beyond the Market Hall the street is now pedestrianised bringing the shops to a virtual standstill. Now the town can only wait the arrival of St George and hope.

GRAND UNION CANAL, UXBRIDGE, c.1955. U52006

The Grand Union Canal was built around 1805, entering the London Borough from the Midlands to the north of Harefield, and passing Uxbridge on its way to Brentford in the south. Although no longer used by the great barges, it is very popular with narrow boat enthusiasts.

HIGH STREET, WALTHAMSTOW, 1904. 51421

Now a well known East London street market, the buildings in the photograph survive, but the shops tend to be used purely as market storage. The elaborate twin-towered Palace theatre in the middle distance was designed by Wilson and Long, who were also architects for the Tottenham Palace, in 1903, but with the death of Variety it was closed in 1954 and demolished in 1960. Only thirty years old, the congregational church in the far distance designed by J Tarring and Son, had not yet lost its spire.

WOOD STREET, WALTHAMSTOW, 1907.   58548
Remarkably this view has changed little. The railway bridge remains, as do the buildings, although traffic numbers have swelled somewhat.

OLYMPIC WAY, WEMBLEY STADIUM, c.1960.   W314029
The twin Wembley towers, an inspiring sporting symbol since the stadium was built in 1923 as part of the British Empire Exhibition. The approach from the underground station as shown in the photograph has changed little since the 1948 London Olympic Games, but in recent years the setting of the stadium, from this viewpoint, has been remodelled. Money well spent? Well, maybe not if the multi-million pound National Stadium rebuilding programme materialises within the foreseeable future.

L130034

LONDON BRIDGE, WESTMINISTER, 1880.
Tremendously noisy iron-tyred wheels pour across the bridge along with crowds of hatted pedestrians. A bridge has been on this site since Roman times, but the photograph shows the superb five arch structure designed by Sir John Rennie (1761-1821), bridge builder of genius. Of buildings in the photograph only the pedimented Fishmongers Hall of 1834 survives. Adelaide House of 1924, a lumpish building by Sir John Burnet and Tate, occupies the left-hand side of the bridge while all others have been replaced. This bridge was sold to the United States in 1967, it is thought, in mistake, for Tower Bridge, and was rebuilt at Lake Havasu City in Arizona,

L130008

PARLIAMENT SQUARE, WESTMINISTER, 1890.
Little has changed, as the camera looks across the square towards the Houses of Parliament and Westminster Hall, except that all is clean and pristine now.

COVENT GARDEN MARKET, 1900.

A wonderful higgledy-piggledy, apparently organised conglomeration of wagons, carts, fruit and vegetable and containers and porters, which were the very life and soul of this area of London until 1974 when the Market moved to its new sanitised home at Nine Elms, south of the river. The market was first established in the garden of Bedford House in 1656; but it was not until early into the nineteenth century that it expanded dramatically. The long, elegant building forming the backdrop to the photograph was erected in the early 1830s to designs by Charles Fowler in the Piazza, in response to a revised Act of Parliament requiring the better organisation of traders. The Floral Hall was opened in 1860, the Flower Market in 1871 and the Jubilee Market in 1904. When the Market decanted to Nine Elms, the buildings were taken over by the much-maligned Greater London Council who with supreme care converted them to small shops, cafés and offices. The recent works on the gargantuan extensions to the Royal Opera House offered archaeologists the rare opportunity to excavate an area of reasonable size in central Westminster, and from not many feet below the surface of the ground emerged an amazing snapshot of Saxon London.

DRURY LANE, WESTMINISTER, 1870.   L130097
This quite amazing photograph was taken some 30 years before the area was totally destroyed in the clearances which made way for the widening of The Strand and the pushing through of the Aldwych Crescent, completed in 1905. The camera looks down Drury Court to St Mary Le Strand, with its wonderful array of seventeenth century and earlier buildings in much the state that Dickens must have seen them on his perambulations through London.

St Giles Circus, Westminister, *c.*1910.
A wonderful selection of buses and cars criss-cross the circus. The camera looks south down Charing Cross Road and what changes have been wrought here in the name of progress. While the photographer stands in front of the Art Deco Dominion theatre, it is the curving building on the left which has disappeared to accommodate Richard Seiferts controversial 36-storey Centre Point office block of 1966, with its windswept, rather gloomy open ground storey.

DANCING BEAR, 1895.   L130108
In an era when animal welfare and animal rights have become paramount, bringing as a by-product animal-free circuses and anti-hunt fervour, the sight of a dancing bear in 1990s' London would be abhorrent. Not so to the children of a century ago, whose faces show only innocent amusement and interest.

CHIMNEY SWEEP, 1884.   L130115
Posed maybe, but nevertheless an evocative photograph recording a dirty working class trade. Only 10 years before, the Chimney Sweeps Act had been passed relating to sweeps and children, in that the sweep be registered by the police to ensure that adequate safety precautions are observed. Tom of *Water Babies* fame was at last afforded protection of a sort.

WESTMINSTER ABBEY, 1908.

The photograph taken from Brad Sanctury, takes in a single sweep from left to right the Clock Tower of Barrys Houses of Parliament, the Commons Parish Church of St Margaret, the west front of Westminster Abbey and the Victoria Tower. The Gothic buildings on the right are by George Gilbert Scott of 1854. Apart from traffic management and a myriad of visitors, little has changed. The Abbey and the Houses of Parliament have been cleaned in recent years, removing their patina of age and now presenting a rather shiny image.

HOUSES OF PARLIAMENT, WESTMINISTER, 1908.

The fire of 1834 completely devastated the Palace of Westminster. For its rebuilding some 97 designs were submitted and the honour went to Charles Barry (1795-1860), who was born locally. His planning of the new palace, combined with a richness of Gothic detail were an inspiration. Internally Barry - who was knighted in 1852 - worked with Augustus Welby Pugin to create a perfectly detailed scheme deriving from the Tudor period. In the photograph, little has changed externally since 1908, but internally much rebuilding was carried out following German bombing raids in 1940 and 1941.

BUCKINGHAM PALACE, *c.*1890.   L130173

It was King George IV who decided on the demolition of Buckingham House, and employed John Nash of Regent Street fame, to design his new palace. The king died before the building was completed and by 1837 it still remained unfinished. Architect, Edward Bloor was appointed to replace Nash and in the photograph is seen his design for the main east front. The present front was added in 1913 by Sir Aston Webb.

TRAFALGAR SQUARE, 1908.   L130152

Pedestrians wander casually in the road, but the overall view looking north has changed little. Nelsons Column, the National Gallery and the church of St Martin-in-the-Fields remain visually intact. Todays visitor would, however, be aware of the Sainsbury wing attached to the National Gallery and designed by American architects Venturi Scott Brown Associates of Philadelphia, which was opened to mixed critical reviews in 1988. The wing occupies the site of Hamptons Furniture Store, which was bombed in 1940.

HIGH STREET, WIMBLEDON, 1959.
W375042

1959 or 1998, the town centre wears the same later nineteenth-century look. New buildings have actually cheered up its slightly deteriorating appearance of the late 1980s. A pleasant town which leaves no lasting memories.

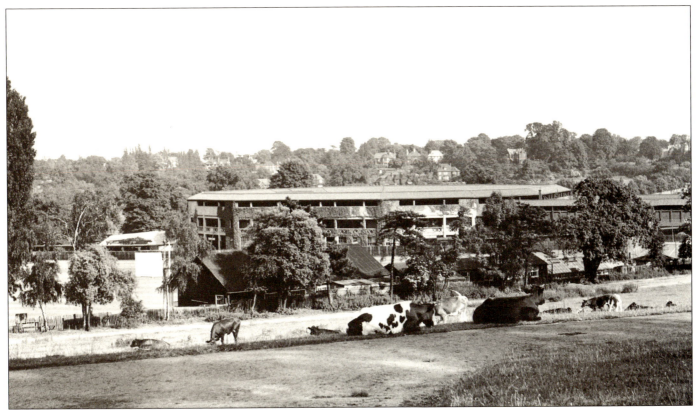

THE CENTRE COURT, WIMBLEDON, c.1950.
W375004

Were it not for the All England Tennis Club, Wimbledon would be just another London suburb, but every year during June, the worlds finest tennis players descent for 'Wimbledon Fortnight'. The buildings and facilities have improved quite considerably over the years since 1950, particularly since the Club accepted professional entrants to the tournament. Prize money escalates, hand in hand with the cost of public entry and strawberries, but still the crowds pour in.

GEORGE LANE, WOODFORD, 1921.
The photograph has a strangely posed air about it but the physical scene has changed little. The buildings of around 1880 remain, minus some of their decoration. The low building is the distance has been replaced by a larger bank and that rare sight, the pawnbrokers' balls, have gone. The picket fence in the foreground marks the entrance to South Woodford railway station.

HIGH ROAD, WOODFORD GREEN, 1921.   70105
A leafy photograph, as the forest leaks into the village, with just the sort of attractive grouping of building that would enhance any main road. Today the same view is hardly recognisable - the buildings on the left are transformed into yet another carpark, the Horse and Well Pub survives, but beyond there is now a car showroom. Unless the visitor needs a drink or to see more cars, this sad remnant is hardly the place to go.

ALEXANDRA PALACE, WOOD GREEN, c.1965.   M298012
The Palace was built to rival Crystal Palace on Sydenham Hill in south London. Former International Exhibition Hall and 'Peoples Palace', the building was rebuilt by John Johnson and Alfred Meeson, 1873-75. It was restored by the Alexandra Palace Development team 1970-75 and again by the team in 1980-88, following a serious fire. Designed in an Italianate style, the building was faced-in with Huntingdon and yellow stock brick on cast iron and steel columns. In 1936, the BBC broadcast the worlds first television programme from here.

BERESFORD SQUARE (MARKET PLACE), WOOLICH, 1963. W460024
Viewed from the former main gateway into the Arsenal, the Square has changed very little. The building, which possess more character than distinction, compliment an area which remains a very active part of the town.

ZOOLOGICAL GARDENS. ALBERT ROAD, WESTMINISTER, 1913. 65252
Since the invention of theme parks and animal rights movement, the magnetism of Regent's Park Zoo seems to have waned. Elephant rides, feeding the penguins and the seals were memorable high points of a child's visit to London, but so much in the capital has changed over the past century.

Pictorial Memories Collection

A great new range of publications featuring the work of innovative Victorian photographer Francis Frith.

	County Series	£9.99			Country Series	£9.99
1-84125-045-7	Berkshire		1-84125-075-9	Ireland	
053-8	Buckinghamshire		071-6	North Wales	
024-4	Derbyshire		073-2	Scotland	
077-5	Greater London		069-4	South Wales	
028-7	Kent				
029-5	Lake District				
051-1	Lancashire			*Poster Books*	£4.99
031-7	Leicestershire				
026-0	London		000-7	Canals and Waterways	
027-9	Norfolk		032-5	Derbyshire	
030-9	Sussex		001-5	High Days and Holidays	
063-5	West Yorkshire		036-8	Kent	
025-2	Yorkshire		037-6	Lake District	
			034-1	London	
	Town & City Series	£9.99	005-8	Railways	
					£5.99
010-4	Brighton & Hove				
015-5	Canterbury		023-6	Canterbury	
079-1	Edinburgh		043-0	Derby	
012-0	Glasgow & Clydeside				
081-3	Norwich				
040-6	York				

A selection of our 1999 programme:
County Series
Devon, Cornwall, Nottinghamshire,
Cheshire, Staffordshire, Warwickshire,
Surrey, Hampshire.

Town and City Series
Bradford, Edinburgh, Nottingham, Bristol, Dublin,
Bath, Matlock, Manchester, Buxton, Maidstone,
Colchester, Leeds.

Also available Address Books & Note Books
Derbyshire, Lake District,
Kent, London.